Unraveling Anne

LAUREL SAVILLE

Unraveling Anne

PUBLISHED BY

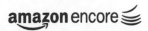

Published by AmazonEncore
P.O. Box 400818
Las Vegas, NV 89140

ISBN-13: 9781612180854
ISBN-10: 161218085X

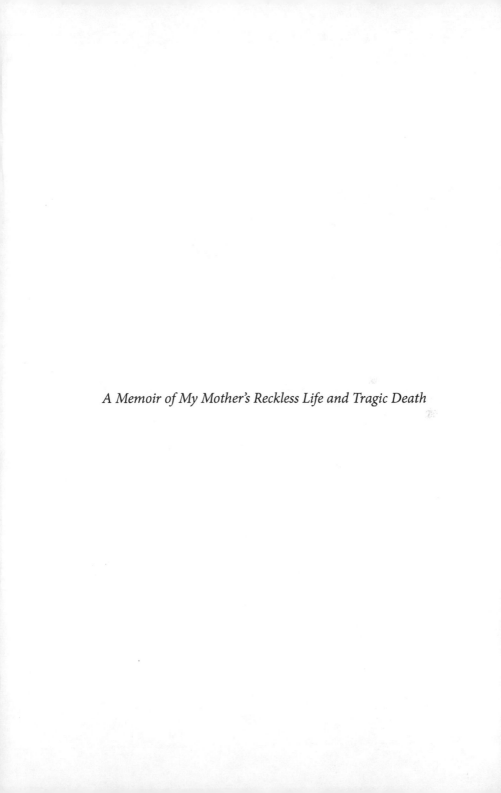

A Memoir of My Mother's Reckless Life and Tragic Death

To Jason for solidarity,
Alice for stories,
Bob for faith,
Gail for tenacity,
Sean for the tightrope walker,
Amanda for close readings,
Terry for going first,
and to Ned for all of the above and everything else.

Author's note: The author's half brother has chosen to appear under a pseudonym in this book.

Contents

$\mathscr{P}$rologue

"Murdered?"

The word always gets repeated. Sometimes the whole sentence. "Your mother was murdered?" As if I could get something like that wrong. As if I could be mistaken.

My mother was murdered.

It's a shocking word, *murdered*. I don't like to use it. But it is the truth. *Murder* is the only word that honestly describes her death. So sometimes, when someone asks what happened to my mother, instead of holding onto this word, toying with the small pain of it as if it were a loose tooth, I go ahead and spit it out. No matter how many times I do, no matter how many people I tell, the raw strangeness of the fact of my mother's death never changes. I try not to watch the people who hear this piece of unexpected news. But I do. I look for the freshness of their surprise, for the way their eyes flicker, their mouth tightens. I watch and wonder what they're thinking, of me and of who my mother was or might have been.

I always feel I need to say more. Like I need to put this information into some kind of understandable context, to explain my mother's life by explaining how she got to her death. I want to help other people assimilate this news, help them get over it, or let them feel they're helping me get over it. I sense I need to reassert myself, to show somehow that I'm the same person, that this news has changed nothing about me, that it should change nothing about who the other person thinks I am.

At the same time, I don't want to explain anything at all. I'm still just a little wearied by the fact that of all the burdens my mother put on me while she was alive, the worst one continues after her death, precisely because of the way she died.

I also don't want to say anything more because I don't feel I have what I imagine are the appropriate emotions to attend to this information, the expected sensations of loss, horror, and sadness. I never have and still don't see either of us as a victim of her murder, or her murderer. I may never fully understand what it means to be the daughter of my mother, much less the daughter of a murdered woman, any more than any of us fully comprehend the myriad ways our parents shaped us.

Sometimes I simply don't want to share this story. After all, this is my mother we're talking about. As her daughter, I belonged to her; as my mother, she also belongs to me. I don't have her anymore, but I still have her story.

More often than not, I simply say that my mother is dead. But then, I feel like I'm lying. Sometimes I say she was killed. But that's dissembling. Other times, I say I don't want to talk about "it," or say, "Some other time. Over a beer or six." But then, I'm hiding something. Not just something about her, but something about me. Sometimes, I don't say anything at all.

It's a long story, the tale of how my mother got to be a woman who was murdered. She had all the raw materials that should have foretold a life of accomplishment and happiness. For a while, she had all these things. But before her life reached a credible apex, it began to dip and then tumble downward. My mother was once a beauty pageant winner, an artist, and a fashion designer. She ended up a bloated, ranting, alcoholic street person, stabbed and strangled in a burned-out building, her sundress hiked up around her waist, her panties caught around an ankle, her ancient, tiny, one-eyed dog standing guard over her body, growling at the police who were called to the scene.

Only, that's not the story I've told people. When I told it at all, I offered a shortened version, a compressed tragedy, complete with rising tension, a heroine with a fatal flaw or two or ten, a denouement of bad choices and worse luck, and then a bloody final scene: a talented, fortunate, beautiful woman is beset with alcoholism and mental illness, which lead her to the streets, and she ends up murdered by another street person. I've told myself that I don't want to burden other people with too many searing and ugly images. I told myself that this abridgement was more than enough.

But because I offered only a superficial synopsis, what I got in return was only the usual platitudes. "All those experiences made you the strong and independent person you are today." "Well, your life is so good now, you can just move on and forget about all that other stuff." "Of course, we all have our troubles." In my younger years, I allowed myself the hot and cold comfort of these small pities, soaked up assurances that these experiences had been somehow all to the good. Strength was my booby prize, a tool made for me at the white-hot forge of life. But as I grew older, I began to feel that these tidy assessments were poison to deeper feelings and more complex understandings.

If I ever really did, I eventually stopped believing that suffering makes you a better person. It simply makes you a person who knows more. And a person who knows more has an equal chance of becoming good, strong, and self-reliant or bitter, withdrawn, and mean. Or anything else, for that matter. I have discovered a more important, more awkward, and less comfortable lesson: there is luck in this world; some of it is good, but plenty of it is bad. My mother had lots of both.

I also no longer believe that a happy present somehow makes past challenges and traumas suspect, somehow not so bad after all. I once thought that the conventional successes I experienced in my life naturally cauterized the wounds of my childhood. But even amputees feel phantom pain. We may choose to pause on the timeline of a life and say, "Things are fine now, right here," but the condition of the present does not change anything—good, bad, or indifferent—about the events that preceded it.

And, I have come to reject the notion that we are all somehow equal under the laws of generalized family dysfunction. One person's absent father is not another person's alcoholic mother. One person's physical abuse is not equivalent to another's neurotic parenting. I think this tendency to caption the complex is an effort to equalize the pressure that builds between people when we discover our assumptions about another are wrong, that so many of the experiences and memories we thought we had in common don't exist, that someone we seemed to know was harboring fundamental differences.

There was a time when talking about my mother meant trying to explain the personality of a very difficult, self-absorbed, unstable alcoholic. Then she was murdered. And she became a woman defined not by how she lived but by how she died. By extension, I became a woman defined not so much by how I lived but by what I survived. Our life stories seemed to represent two neatly opposing arcs: she had all the advantages parents could offer or a child could want, but, after a point, her life's progression began to move in reverse. In turn, I took the chaos and danger of my childhood and turned it into a life filled with the usual accomplishments, along with the petty and comprehensible failures of a typical, college-educated, middle-class, socially conscious, liberal-leaning, culturally aware, married then divorced then happily remarried professional. For many years, this equation made sense to me. It was enough for me. But eventually, I began to realize that this summary not only was a pallid shortcut through a complicated life but also left me with a paucity of feeling and understanding for my mother. And, even more important, for myself.

I never really had my mother. For a variety of reasons, she held herself at bay from me. I, in turn, spent much of my early life avoiding her, distancing myself from her emotionally, psychologically, and, eventually, physically. But I have always had her story. Or, at least, the broken bits and pieces of it that were passed down to me. Over time, I began to realize that it was my story, too. I began to see that by avoiding her, I avoided parts of myself. As I got older, these spectral aspects of my left-behind self reared their heads from time to time, startling me with the ache of their presence. I wondered not only where these sensations went but also where they came from. Within every ghostly vision of some neglected or rejected part of myself, I saw the shadow of my mother. I began to feel there were three women I wanted to know better: my mother as I knew her, my mother as the person she was before I knew her, and myself. I began to want to know, to understand, the complete story of who my mother was, how she became the woman she was, and what her story might mean for my own.

Safety

This is one of my earliest memories.

It is 1968. Or maybe 1969. My mother and I are on our way home from my half day of kindergarten, walking west down the eight or nine blocks of Sunset Boulevard between Gardner Street Elementary School and our house on the corner of Fairfax Avenue. The midday sun is high, reflecting off the white concrete, the white stucco buildings, the smoggy particles in the air. My mother loves this temperature, this dissipated light, so distinct to Southern California. I find it an affront, a glary, squint-inducing assault.

On this day, this walk home, as usual I am trying to keep up with my mother's long stride, trotting for a few steps and then dragging for a few, my hand sweaty and slippery in hers, even though the tips of her magenta-colored fingernails are digging into the back of my hand. I am simultaneously whining and trying very hard not to whine. I know I irritate her enough when I don't make any noise at all, but I am worn down by the hours at school, the heat, and the on-alert, watchful feeling I always have when I am with her.

We come to a side street and pause at the curb. A large, dark car comes down the street, slows, pulls up, and stops. We wait. The car doesn't proceed out onto Sunset. The window rolls down to reveal a black-haired, middle-aged, somewhat attractive man smiling at us. My mother smiles back. I know this without even looking up. I know how she responds to the attention of men. I can feel it in how she slightly shifts her posture, adjusts the angle of her shoulders.

I, perverse child that I am, frown at him.

The man says, "Would you two pretty ladies like a ride?"

He is looking at my mother with desire disguised as friendliness. I am already accustomed to watching men look at my mother this way. The man glances at me, and his expression does not change. I am not won over. I know that he sees me simply as part of the path to her. Once, not long before this incident, a man I'd never seen before appeared at our front door with a dozen yellow roses, and when I said I'd bring them to my mother, he smiled and said, no, no, they were for me—the whole time looking over my shoulder at her coming down the stairs.

I know the only thing I have that this man, that any man, wants is my mother. I already know that she is a beautiful woman, and I am just a pretty little girl; I am beginning to suspect just how large and various the implications of this difference may be.

My mother doesn't say anything to the man in the car. Not yet. She tilts her head, lifts the corners of her mouth, and lowers her eyes. This is the thing she does with men. This is how it starts. Her large gray-blue eyes look down at me from behind the layers of mascara, black eyeliner, colored shadow.

"Lolly," she says, loud enough for the man to hear, her voice a breathy singsong. "Would you like a ride?"

She asks me this in the tone adults use when they want a child to say yes. I think about my kindergarten teacher, Mrs. Jackson of the sensible shoes, the simple dresses, the neat handwriting, the straightforward rules and ready rewards, telling us that we should never accept a ride from a stranger. I remember her telling us another time that we might see a man parked near the schoolyard who might offer us candy to get into his car and that we should never accept but come tell her right away, so she could call the police. Even if my teacher had never told us those things, my answer would be the same. I am far too shy, too suspicious of strangers in general and men in particular, to accept this offer of a ride, no matter how much the incessant heat from the hard sidewalk penetrates my shoes and makes my feet ache.

I shake my head no.

"But you're so hot and uncomfortable. Wouldn't you like a ride for the last few blocks?" my mother says, her voice cajoling as it comes through the smile on her pink-lipsticked mouth.

I set my lips in stubborn refusal. I know I am risking her anger. But I don't like this situation, this man, men in general. Their longing for her, their forward approaches when we are in the grocery store or walking down the street or at a party. Saying no, digging in my heels, is the only way I have yet discovered to defend myself from these games the adults play. It is my only trick. So I use it again and again.

I shake my head and look at the pavement. I grip her hand harder.

My mother shrugs with a feigned helplessness and says to the man, "I guess not today. Thanks, anyway."

He nods and drives away, looking over his shoulder once or twice. She smiles and waves. I know I have not really won this battle. Her polite acquiescence to my refusal was a performance for the man, not a concession to me, my feelings, my more cautious approach to the world. She turns to me, her expression now suddenly dark, looks into my face, and tells me I'm being silly for not taking the ride. She says I'd better stop complaining, now. That I always wreck everything for her, I never want to have any fun.

She is gone from me. She has taken herself away to some brooding place inside herself that I cannot reach. But then again, so have I. We walk on in silence.

When we get to the next side street, there is a car stopped in the intersection. It takes me a moment to realize it is the same car, the same man. Now he is watching us approach, his elbow out the window, his eyes eager. This time, he doesn't look at me at all, only at my mother, hungry, insistent.

"I'll give you fifty dollars to get in the car with me," he says.

She stands a bit taller, my mother, raising her chin out in front of her face. She looks at him carefully. She has just the smallest of smiles on her face. She shakes her head, assumes a tone of cautious deference I am not used to hearing, and says, very demurely, "No. No thank you."

A shadow crosses his face, but he drives away.

He is there at the next corner. He suggests more money. This time, my mother does not look at him, just gives her head a few firm shakes side to side.

I don't remember how many more corners he met us at, but I do remember that the amount he offered increased each time. My mother quickened her step. I jogged alongside, my lips pressed together.

"We'll beat him to the next corner," she said, her voice eager for the chase.

My mother was deft at turning the things I found dangerous into a game. We jogged down the block. There was no long, dark car waiting for us.

"See," she said. "Everything's fine."

Then, after trotting down another block, we were home.

"That was exciting, wasn't it?" she said.

She claimed victory, even where there had been only luck. She took credit for beating opponents who simply grew tired of playing. She attracted danger and then flirted shamelessly with it.

I squinted up at her against the harsh afternoon light, my eyes stinging with the smog, my hand damp with nerves, and wondered if I'd be able to save her—to save us both—the next time.

The Hollywood Homicide Bureau

I knew the Hollywood Homicide Bureau was only a few blocks from where my mother had lived on Hudson Avenue, just off Sunset Boulevard. Where I once lived with her, I reminded myself, as I always had to do when I thought of the end of her life.

My brother and I had walked past the police station many times when we were twelve and thirteen years old, on our way to and from the seedy grocery store over on Vine. When the kitchen was completely empty of food, we'd scrape together some change, swipe a few bills from her wallet, walk to the store, and pick up a quart of milk, a loaf of bread, a couple of tins of tuna, a few cartons of yogurt. We'd count our money as we walked down the aisles to avoid the embarrassment of not having enough when we got to the checkout counter. I remember trading the heavy grocery bag between us as we walked home past buildings with bright red and yellow bail bond signs.

That was in 1975. Twenty-one years had passed since I had been on these streets. I was now thirty-two years old. I drove down Sunset, past the concrete buildings of Hollywood High where my brother went to school and where I would have gone had I stayed in Los Angeles instead of moving back East.

I drove a few more blocks and took a right onto Hudson Avenue. I pulled over to the curb and looked for the front porch with the creaking swing where I used to find my mother, or someone else, passed out at night. I looked for the jacaranda trees she planted between the sidewalk and the street because she craved their clusters of blue flowers. I looked for the side yard with its long line of rosebushes.

But there was nothing there.

As I sat there in my stepmother's rattling old Honda, I suffered from a strange lag of comprehension. I knew the house had been badly burned fifteen or so years earlier when someone had thrown a torch into the garage. I knew that, in spite of the holes in the walls and ceiling, the lack of utility service, my mother had continued living in it, off and on, when she wasn't in her car or camping at the beach or at the empty lot she'd somehow acquired in Ventura. I had thought, without really realizing it, that someone would have bought the house and renovated it, restored the hand-carved woodwork, spruced up the yard. But there was nothing there except an expansion of the parking lot attached to an office building on Sunset.

Before I moved back East when I was thirteen years old, when I didn't want to be in the house with my mother and the men she attracted, I would come out at night to that parking lot and bang a tennis ball against the side of that office building. I remembered the soothing feeling and satisfaction of the steady, repeated thwacking, over and over again, ball, wall, racket, wall, waiting, hoping that the men would leave, my mother would fall asleep, and I could find my way to my room where I'd be safe until morning when I could go back to school.

Now, the garage, just barely big enough to hold her Volkswagen Bug, was gone. The tiny backyard with the low, ivy-covered, chain-link fence and gate that faced the next street over was gone. The lemon tree she'd sit under and the pond she'd built—taking the fragments from a drawer full of broken plates and glasses and pressing them into the wet concrete she troweled into the shallow hole she'd gotten some friend to dig for her—was gone. I'd heard that she'd gotten in trouble with the city for that pond. Ducks had arrived, unbidden, began to nest, ducklings appeared, and neighbors complained that she was "harboring" wildlife. In spite of the degradations of her own life, she went to court to protect those birds. To let them live freely, where they wanted. She enjoyed disputing with the neighbors, thumbing her nose at authority. It was a point of pride with her, as she saw herself as terminally persecuted and misunderstood by people who were "uptight."

To her, I was one of those people. From earliest childhood, my personality was an affront to her and her way of life. She called me a "drag" and a "bore." Among other, harsher, viler things.

The street seemed very peaceful to me, now. No one was standing on the front porch, screaming at me. Nearby, rosebushes peeked out of chain-link fencing in front of compact bungalows. Grass was in short supply in the small, dry yards. Exuberant bougainvillea vines softened the silent, two-story, pale-colored, stucco apartment buildings. The sidewalks were chalk-whitened in the sun. I pulled away from the curb and drove on.

At the corner, there was a familiar low brick wall that surrounded another paved lot and a set of garages where police cars were kept and maintained. My mother used to wave to the mechanics as she walked by and talk about how cute they looked in their blue uniforms with their bulging muscles. Every day that I walked past this lot on my way to Bancroft Junior High School, I looked away, mortified.

At the stop sign, I turned the Honda to the left, and then at the next corner, to the right. The homicide bureau should be on Wilcox, the next block. I'd looked up the address before I left, just to be sure. But again, something had changed, and I couldn't find the building.

I looked at the numbers scribbled on the sheet of paper in my sweaty palm. I looked back at the buildings, but the numbers seemed out of sequence. I drove by and turned around at the next corner, came back, and still couldn't find the building. I turned again and parked across the street from where the police station was supposed to be. I stared out the car window, and, finally, a squat building became apparent behind the low-hanging branches of an overgrown tree, which, of course, would have been much smaller when I walked by as a child some twenty years earlier.

Through the shadows, I saw wide, concrete stairs leading to a set of double glass doors. Through the screen of leaves, I saw numbers that matched those written on the scrap of paper in my trembling hand.

I took some deep breaths. To steady myself, I remembered my home in the countryside, three thousand miles away, where

9

my dogs and gardens waited for me. I remembered that there, I had a good job, plenty of friends; there I was liked, considered fun, good-humored, full of energy, quick to laugh, always up for an event or an adventure, independent-minded, a risk taker, even. It was only here, in this place, in this city, that my mood turned dark, and I became, again, the humorless, self-protected, serious child I once was. I asked myself why I had come, why I was putting myself through this, what I had hoped to find. I didn't know the answers to those questions, but I did know that I was tired of hearing about my mother's life and death from other people, who for good reason didn't want to recount what they knew, what they'd witnessed. I wanted to see for myself whatever was left to see.

* * *

More than a dozen years earlier, in November 1983, I had been standing in the darkened kitchen of a chilly farmhouse in central New Jersey that belonged to my father and stepmother, trying to spread some hard butter on dry toast when the phone rang. I was a senior in college at New York University and living in their house, which my father had started to renovate but had left incomplete. They had just moved back to California and were trying to decide if they were going to stay out West and if my dad would like this new job as the head of a commercial interior design group. He was uncomfortable, as usual, working for someone else, being accountable to other people, other methods, and having young people with more education and experience working for him. The security of not having his own business, not chasing jobs, and having a steady paycheck with benefits didn't seem to outweigh the discomfort, what he called his "fear of being found out."

I was commuting to two long days of classes and working on the other days and holidays at a decent job in an office, writing content for databases, supporting myself, and paying for college. It was past dinnertime, and as I often didn't eat during the day as a cost-saving measure, I was hungry, making something quick to fill my empty stomach and trying to decide whether it was worth firing up the potbellied stove to heat the house or if I should just eat, crawl under some blankets, and read myself to sleep.

The ring of the phone startled me. I picked it up and said hello.

"Lolly?"

Almost no one used my childhood nickname anymore. I'd asked the few family members who called me that to stop, back when I was eleven years old. Everyone other than my mother had. But this was not her voice. This voice sounded like it was coming over a string that had been pulled too taut.

"Grandma?" I said. "Is that you?"

"Yes. Yes. Lolly, how are you, dear?" Her voice, normally upbeat and expressive, was a rustling of dry leaves.

"I'm OK, Grandma. But how are you? You don't sound well. What's wrong?"

"No, I'm fine," she said. I could hear her swallow before she added, "It's your mother."

I took in a breath. Of course, I thought. It's always my mother.

"What, Grandma? What has she done? What's going on?"

She stuttered and stumbled and then choked out, "She's gone, Lolly. She's gone."

"Gone where, Grandma?" I asked stupidly, impatient, thinking she'd simply disappeared again and would turn up at my grandmother's back door, dirty, looking for a shower and a meal, after having been kicked off some beach in Malibu where she'd been "camping" for a few weeks.

My grandmother didn't answer me. Her breathing was strained.

I tried again.

"Grandma," I said. "What do you mean? How long has she been gone?"

"No. I don't know." She was drifting; her voice trailed away and then came back. "The police. The police came by…Jason. Jason was here," she managed. "But he's gone now. I told him I'd call you. They said.…"

The police?

My brother, Jason, had mentioned that our mother had been arrested for vagrancy a couple of times in the preceding year or so. But he'd also mentioned that she'd been living back in the Hudson house. She'd mentioned it herself in a letter.

"Grandma, what happened? What did the police say?" I tried to make my voice gentle. She was stumbling over words and phrases that were too big to find her way around, too huge to comprehend. She was in her eighties then. I was more concerned for her than for my mother.

"They said something…they said she was…a pillow…he used a pillow." Her voice sped up into a choked wail and then sputtered, "She's gone, Lolly. He killed her. Suffocated her. Someone found her. At the house."

I swallowed hard and clenched my teeth against this news.

"Grandma, are you OK? Are you alone? Grandma, is anyone with you?"

"Yes. No. I'm OK." A pause. Then, "Are you OK? Is anyone with you?"

"I'm fine, Grandma. I'm fine."

There was quiet between us.

"Grandma, I'm going to go now," I said distinctly. "I'll call Jason. I'll call you again later. Grandma, you go sit down. You go take care of yourself. I'll call you soon."

I hung up the phone, put my face into my hands, then looked up at the raw ceiling and said, aloud, to the cold, dark house, "That bitch. She couldn't even make this easy."

* * *

The following days were blurry with tears and telephone calls—my brother, my father, my grandmother, a cousin of my mother, my boyfriend. Some friends came by and tried to sit with me, to get me to eat, to talk, neither of which I wanted to do. One friend made me dinner of roasted leeks and pork loin, fed me sweet liquor warmed in the ashes from a dying fire, and thereby gave me my first bad hangover.

There were few details to gather. My mother had been stabbed and strangled in an upstairs bedroom of her fire-damaged home. Some guy who'd been sleeping on the porch for a few days had found her. There were no suspects; it could have been any one of the various homeless people and drifters who wandered in and out of the house.

"You know how she was," my brother said, an often-used shorthand.

I did. And I didn't. But I knew what he meant.

He arranged a service. I didn't want to go. I thought I knew everything I needed to know about my mother's life and death.

13

I thought I didn't want to see the remnants of the artists, hippies, musicians, vagabonds, and drifters who had cluttered my childhood stand up and say what they often had: how wonderful my mother had been, what a talent, what a creative soul, what a misunderstood person who had always been ahead of her time. Their words described a woman I had never seen, a woman who didn't exist for me and had never chosen to shine the bright light of her charms or talents toward me—her youngest child and the penultimate "drag" in her life. I thought I would mourn her in my own time, my own way. I thought it wouldn't take very long, as I had mourned her through so much of my life already. I thought I was, in many ways, already over it. I was only twenty years old. I didn't, I couldn't, know that her death would be not the end of my relationship with her but in many ways just the beginning.

* * *

Some months after my mother's death, I called the detective who handled her case. My brother and I always knew she'd end up badly—we just never knew how badly. Now that she was dead, there was nothing in particular either of us wanted to do or wanted done, other than to get on with our lives, finish college, move forward. But I was curious. I wanted to know if anything had come up, if there were any leads, what might happen next. I expected an officially detached recounting from a hardened, overworked detective assigned a throwaway case about a throwaway person. What I got instead was a sympathetic voice softened by regret, laced with resignation. He told me that they'd investigated the case, but there were no witnesses, no murder weapon, and only one suspect who'd been questioned and released. It was, unfortunately, a street crime, he said.

She died the way she lived, I thought. Then I said it aloud.

"We all knew your mother," the detective said, his voice muted by memory. "The neighbors would call us with complaints about her parties." There was not even a whiff of rancor in his voice. "We all called her Crazy Annie."

I winced, but at my memories, not his. I asked if the case was now closed. He said that cases are never closed, but shelved, moved to the inactive pile, where this one was. Something might come up, he said. Someone could come in on a different charge and say, "Hey, I know who killed that Annie Ford," in an effort to use that information for bargaining. It could be months, it could be years. It could be never.

Or, as I learned ten years after her death, more than fifteen years after leaving her house for the last time, it could be pure luck. I had gotten fragments of some information from my brother, who was always reluctant to talk about our mother, to deal with the emotional agony discussing her conjured up, especially for he who had been her darling, her beloved, who lived with her longer and cared for her more than I had. Even though I was the family outcast, I always considered his position of greater entanglement much more difficult than mine. Once he finally became free of her, I avoided dragging him back to confront painful memories. So when he told me that they'd "found the guy who killed Mom," as stunned as I was, I tried not to ask him a lot of questions.

The next day, sitting in my office at work, my door closed, I watched colleagues walk up and down the hallway outside my windows, coffee cups in hand, while I placed another phone call to the Hollywood Homicide Bureau, stumbled out my story about my mother having been murdered ages ago, finding out they'd charged someone, wondering if I could get more information.

15

The man who picked up the phone had answered in a growl. Before I could even finish my jumbled story, he changed his tone. He called me "hon." He asked me to slow down. I leaned into the solidity of his voice and repeated myself. He asked me my mother's name.

"Anne Jacqueline Ford."

There was a dead moment on the line.

"Annie?" he said. "Annie Ford?"

I didn't like the diminutive form of her name. I didn't understand the incredulity in his voice.

"Yes," I said. "Anne Ford."

"I'm the one who handled her case," he said.

Somehow, out of all the detectives at the bureau, the one who solved her case happened to be at his desk, happened to pick up the ringing phone with me on the other end. And then he told me what had happened in a voice pitched for the telling of bad news: low and lightly guarded with the fear that the person listening might become excessively emotional.

He couldn't have known this, but I wasn't about to get emotional. My feelings for my mother had been all twisted and dried up in the hot winds of her life. Besides, I'd already had a lot of bad news in the previous year or so. Divorce, financial setbacks, job changes, my father diagnosed with an inoperable brain tumor. I felt like a shrub that had been radically pruned, and I was waiting to see what might grow back, what new form my life might take. I listened to the words and the rhythms of the detective's voice and let the information soak into me like a cup of water slowly poured into dry ground.

In fact, he didn't have much to say: just that he'd been assigned to review the old case and discovered that a homeless drifter who had been questioned right after the murder and then let go for insufficient evidence had been arrested on another matter and was being held at a different police station. Because he'd been an original suspect, detectives had showed him a picture of my mother and he had said, "Yeah, I remember that lady. I don't know why I hurt her." He had then gone on to say other things that only the person who pushed a small knife into her chest and wrapped his large hands around her throat could have known. He was charged, but because he was not only violent but also mentally unfit, he was locked up as criminally insane. He did not stand trial. The case was closed. For the detective, anyway. I didn't know what else I wanted to know—just that I wanted to know more. I didn't know what I expected to find—just that I wanted to see the evidence rather than hearing about it from someone else. So I told him I had plans to be in Los Angeles soon. Could I come by the station? Could I look at the casebook? He said there wasn't much more to tell me, but he'd be happy to show me the book. He told me to call and to expect that he'd be hard to reach. He never knew when he might be called out to a case, to court.

My father's birthday was coming up. My stepmother had asked my brother, my stepbrother, and me, all of us now in our early thirties, to come to Los Angeles, to put aside whatever emotional injuries we harbored from the past and to simply try to be together on what was clearly going to be his last birthday. There was no treatment for this kind of tumor, lodged on his brain stem, inoperable. He'd already lived longer than the doctors had expected; they'd tried everything they had to slow the growth. The drugs were damaging him in other ways. We were all waiting, we'd all tried to talk to him about his coming to the end of his life, but my father always had a tenuous relationship with the truth, and he was encased in a denial so deep his doctor said she'd never encountered anything like it in all her years of practice.

I made an appointment with the detective for my last day in Los Angeles. I didn't want to carry around the extra weight of whatever additional news I had about my mother while I was trying to navigate the strange and shifting territory that was my father's alternately hostile and childlike behavior toward me. I was trying to find some way of saying good-bye to him without tainting my efforts to find some trace of her.

For three days, I kept encouraging my father to do something with me, take a walk, go to a museum, sit on the beach, talk. He evaded me with an assiduousness that was so blatant and baffling it left both my stepmother and me speechless; she shook her head and mouthed words of apology on his behalf. I couldn't blame the brain tumor because his recent behavior, although exaggerated, was so distinctly my father's own. The tumor seemed to be annealing every trick he'd ever developed to maintain his advanced level of self-protection. Yet the morning of my appointment at the police station, as I was finishing a cup of tea, checking my watch, discussing the eccentricities of my stepmother's old car, my father emerged from his room and cheerfully asked if I didn't want to go somewhere, to do something "fun" on this, my last day in Los Angeles.

"But, Dad, I told you, remember, I'm going to visit the detective who handled Mom's case."

"Well, I just thought," he huffed, his voice larded with sarcasm, "you *might* like to do something with *me*."

"But, Dad," I pleaded while my stepmother cringed in the background, "I've been asking to do something with you every day I've been here, and you've never wanted to. And now, I have this appointment that I can't miss. I told you about this all along. This is my last chance to see the detective."

He looked at me as if I were something dirty he'd stepped in. "Well, they're only going to give you, like, five minutes, you know that, don't you?"

I shook my head. I told him I was sorry. That I'd get back as soon as I could and maybe we could do something together in the afternoon. My stepmother gave me the keys to her car, and I left my dying father to keep an appointment with my long-dead mother.

* * *

The front of the police station was tree-darkened. I climbed the few steps, pulled open the door, and faced an even gloomier interior. I stood for a moment waiting for my eyes to adjust. Benches lined the walls. And people lined the benches. Chins cupped in hands, elbows on knees, they sat with the listless and bored expressions of those accustomed to waiting, to being ignored, to being put upon and jerked around. I was on guard and adopted an exterior calm that sought to mask my interior agitation. It was a feeling so familiar to me from my childhood that I would not have been able to name it or isolate it. Finally, here, now, again, as an adult, I recognized it as fear for my own safety. As I walked down the long room, eyes followed me, watching for no other reason than there was nothing else to look at. I asked a woman at the front desk for the detective.

"I have an appointment," I added, as if my grooming and attire didn't already distinguish me enough from someone coming in off the street.

She said she'd check. I stood at the counter, not wanting to look around the room, not wanting to rest my eyes on anything, as if I might catch something. She came back. He wasn't here. He was at court. He'd warned me this might happen, but still, I didn't want to leave. Because then I'd just have to come back. She didn't know when he'd be done, she said. Her voice was not helpless, not sorry, just factual. It could be hours.

It was.

I drove away and came back two more times. Finally, a behemoth of a man with red hair, a florid face, and gray pants pulled up high over the mound of his belly came through a door behind the counter and reached down from his substantial height to give me a meaty hand. He looked nervous. Or at least uncomfortable. He seemed unsure where to take me. He led me into a room where a dozen desks were jammed cheek by jowl and men laughed or hunched over phones or tapped haltingly at typewriters. I felt like I'd stepped into a crowded locker room. The detective made a sudden left turn and ushered me into a narrow space that had clearly once been a closet. I sat on a hard metal chair. He said he'd be right back. He disappeared for a few moments and then brought in a four-inch-thick black binder, which he set in front of me before perching his bulk onto the other chair. He partially closed the door. The space moved in around me as if I had crawled under a blanket.

"This is the casebook," he said. "It provides all the details of the investigation." He sighed. "Take your time with it."

I pulled the heavy book toward me and opened the cover. The first inch or so was typed pages. A synopsis at the front. Details of who was interviewed, what they said, what steps were taken. There was a lot of information about the man who had bought my mother's house, told her she could continue living there, then never paid her and kicked her out, eventually letting her back in several months before she was killed. A player, a shady character,

20

but not a killer. There was too much to read, especially under the watchful eye of the detective. I skimmed. Then I started to flip to the back.

"Wait," he said. "Just a minute." He pulled the book toward him and turned over pages until he got to the plastic sleeves that held photos. He tilted the book away from me, looked at a few sheets, and then slid it back to me.

"It's not that I want to keep anything from you...," he said.

"It's just that there are some things I do not need to see," I said, finishing the sentence for him.

He nodded, his face grave, thankful.

I saw pictures of rooms that had once been notable for their elaborate woodwork, now marked by the black haze of smoke damage and the chaotic litter of transient lives. A hall badge from my grammar school days peeked out from among a pile of torn clothing, glittery costume jewelry, an empty cup, some garbage on the floor. Pieces of furniture I had sat or napped in as a child were lopsided and broken as if stone drunk.

There were spaces where the black paper stared out at me from behind empty sleeves. Photos had been removed. The pictures of the body, the victim, the deceased, my mother, the pictures that showed her as they had found her. I understood why he'd removed them. But the truth was, as vivid as my imagination fueled by my own experiences made the last moments of my mother's life, I wanted the pictures, I wanted to see just how bad things had gotten. I wanted the evidence. The detective thought he was protecting me by removing them; in fact, I was protecting him by not asking for them.

There was one picture of her, which he had not removed. It was an eight-by-ten, full-color glossy. The detective told me this photo had been taken months before her death when she had come into the police station to report having been raped and beaten. I vaguely recalled her voice on the phone telling me an incoherent story about being roughed up, but I couldn't get the details straight. For years, she had frequently spoken of being "under attack." I would beg her to tell me what she was talking about, to be specific.

She always said, "Oh, Lolly, it's just too complicated to explain. You blew it. You're missing it all."

She's punishing me, I would tell myself, for not being there.

In the photo in the casebook, my mother's face was scrubbed clean. Her eyebrows were plucked, and her smooth black hair was marked only by scattered ghostly strands of gray. She was staring straight into the camera, her blue eyes faded, but her expression proud, challenging, defiant really.

I looked into her face and started adding things up: at the time the picture was taken, my mother had been living for about six years on and off the streets, in her damaged house, or in her car. She had been drinking large quantities of cheap red wine and smoking a pack of unfiltered cigarettes every day—or as often as she could get her hands on the stuff—for more than twenty years. She had not had regular meals or health care or showers or other basic niceties for more than five years. Her mind was deeply deteriorated from all the ways that her life had exacerbated its inherent flaws.

But before all this, my mother was Miss Redondo Beach, Miss Legs, a Fiesta Queen, a model, a fashion designer, a glamorous girl-about-town. She knew how to take a good picture. And in this picture, she's posing. In this picture, the purples, blacks, blues, and reds that in another part of her life might have been makeup came instead from a huge bruise that spilled over her right eye and cheek. In spite of everything, the photo showed a handsome, some would say beautiful, woman who looked as much as a decade younger than her fifty-three years.

I thought: the most striking thing about my mother is not that she was murdered but that she survived her own life for as long as she did.

There was also a photo of the man who murdered my mother. He stared out at me with black eyes set over the copper-colored cliffs of his cheekbones. I tried to find something in those eyes. They were a long, dark, dead end.

"He's a sociopath," the detective said, looking at me looking at the picture.

If I had seen this man walking toward me, I thought, I would have crossed the street. I imagined my mother seeing him. She would have smiled, turned her head to accentuate her jawline, dropped her shoulders, walked directly toward him, and made a flirtatious remark. She would have looked into this face and seen only a young, strikingly handsome man with long, smooth, black hair, adobe-colored skin, and arresting eyes, who had the potential to remind her of what it was to feel desirable.

I told the detective I was amazed at the thoroughness of the investigation. He nodded, shrugged. I didn't say, but I did think that it was an awful lot of work for one crazy, self-destructive street lady. Who also happened to be my mother. Then I thought, everyone is someone's mother. Or son or daughter. Even the man who killed her. Even me. I asked the detective about the family of the man who killed her. I asked what kind of people they were. He said they were good, solid, hardworking, that they knew their son was trouble and had tried to have him locked up in the past. He said they followed the investigation closely and were relieved he was off the streets. I was glad to hear this and wondered what kinds of demons haunted their thoughts—worse than mine, probably. He was the perpetrator, and we were, technically, the victims. Although I didn't see my mother, or myself, as a victim of the life she led.

I wondered, not for the first time, how it was that bad people came from good people, and good people came from bad people, and why we bother to try to understand the difference. Then, I wondered about the detective, his plain wedding band, the kindness he showed me, what questions his wife asked him when he got home at the end of the day, if he thought about people like me, or if that kind of thinking would make it impossible for him to do his job. I wondered how long you could stick with work like his, where the lines between the good guys and the bad guys are supposed to be clear but must be sometimes so hard to find; and even if you do, there's so little you can do about it, even though you're well over six feet tall and have a badge and a gun and the full force of the law behind you. I wondered if he noticed how much my face mirrored that of the "victim."

Then, I wondered what it felt like to have a knife slipped into your flesh, and I imagined that at first, it probably didn't hurt too much, more like a surprising, small gasp of cool air some place where it's not supposed to be. I wondered about being strangled, and I imagined that would be scary, the gradual cutting off of air to your lungs, the crushing of your windpipe. I wondered what it would feel like to get mad at someone, not too mad, more annoyed and irritated than enraged, and pull a knife out of your pocket or pick it up off a table and press it into the annoyance's flesh—how would you decide where to stick it in, how much force would it take, what would you be thinking might happen next? Then, because you're still irritated, you wrap your fingers around the other person's neck, and squeeze and squeeze until he or she is quiet.

24

Then you leave. Throw the knife away in the bushes or the gutter. Maybe a dog comes by, sniffs at the blade, tests the blood with its tongue. You go on doing all those small tasks of staying alive. And then I wondered how any of us, any of the living, survive the dead.

But it was time for me to leave. The detective had other bad guys to catch, other mysteries whose resolutions were not complete. I took a copy of the summary police report and the detective's business card.

He told me to call him anytime. If I had questions.

I wondered if he knew that the only questions I had left were ones that had no answers.

* * *

I took the police report home to my father's house; the next day I said good-bye to him for the last time and flew back across the country. I put the report in the bottom drawer of an old desk that was not quite an antique but an elegant piece of furniture, nonetheless. The desk sat in the corner of a room with dark green walls, wide pine floors, and a bay window surrounded by substantial moldings. That room was on the first floor of a pale yellow Victorian farmhouse, a house I renovated with my then-husband, a house that had all the picturesque touches like a porch and porch swing, stone walls and walks, perennial gardens, trellises, a large expanse of green lawn. That house sat on five acres of meadow and woods, on a dirt road in a quiet town with polite and helpful neighbors who occasionally argued but over not much more than dogs that barked too early in the morning or whether we should spend tax dollars to install sidewalks. That town is in Vermont, a bucolic and idealized state of mountains and farms that has one of the lowest crime rates in the country.

The friends I had when I lived at that house had all attended reputable colleges, drove nice cars, had garages full of expensive toys disguised as equipment for things like sliding down snow-covered mountains, gliding over lakes, or spinning through wooded trails. We ate meals made with ingredients like free-range chicken, tarragon, balsamic vinegar, and *chèvre*, things we picked up at the co-op or our local Community Supported Agriculture farm stand. Over a few glasses of wine, we talked about our jobs as planners, administrators, managers, lawyers, financial advisers, and consultants, what books we had recently read or movies we saw, perhaps some politics if the subject wasn't too controversial and our opinions were close enough to not cause contention or discomfort. If we were feeling bold, or the hour was late, or we'd opened just one more bottle of chardonnay, we might have discussed our frustrations and disappointments in our relationships, our jobs, our lives. Occasionally we talked of death, when disease had taken someone's grandparents or parents. We'd express sadness at the loss, ask one another how those left behind were "doing."

Sometimes, as I passed the lemon tart, or listened to people complain about the innumerable stresses they faced in the building of their million-dollar homes, or tripped over a hunting dog on my way to the guest bathroom adorned with precious soaps in the shape of shells or flowers and linen towels too clean and pressed to be sullied by human hands, I would pause, swallow against the inexplicable, ill-timed memories of that small, gray room at the Hollywood Homicide Bureau, and ask myself: Where in this life is there a place for a once-beautiful, talented woman who suffocated and bled to death, alone, in a burned-out building with her sundress hiked up around her waist and her panties caught around an ankle? Where, in this life, is there a place for the girl who watched her mother throw herself down the steep ravine of life and somehow managed to keep herself from tumbling after? Where is there space within the grown-up I have become for all the things that the girl I once was knows?

I had no answer. I wanted to be polite, not spoil the mood, not pollute anyone else's mind with ugly images, so I would shake my hands dry so as not to crease the towels, or pour another glass of wine for someone, or simply chew down the acrid sweetness of the lemon tart and my own feelings, and tell myself that that was then and this is now and my life had become all the things the little girl I once was had hoped for, dreamed for, complete with the green hills and the farm animals I used to read about in my mother's childhood copy of *Heidi*. I had loved that book, longed for the life of the child who was sent away—or perhaps escaped—to live quietly among the gentle mountain meadows and goats. Wasn't that just what I had done? All the way down to the detail of the goats, which my father kept for a few years in the barn of our beat-up farmhouse in New Jersey.

Sometimes, after the dinner party had passed and in the empty hours of a quiet Sunday afternoon, if I was digging through that antique desk in the dark green study looking for something benign like a card on which to write a thank-you note to send to my hostess, I might come across a particular manila envelope. If I was feeling brave, I might open that envelope and reread the crime report I brought home with me from the small, gray room at the Hollywood Homicide Bureau:

On 11-3-83, at approximately 1930 hours, the dead body of Anne Saville, F/W, 53 years, was discovered in her second floor bedroom...the cause of death was ascribed to a

27

single stab wound to the chest and manual strangulation. Detectives interviewed the surrounding neighbors of the Saville residence and were informed of the Victim's lifestyle. Saville's mental state had deteriorated over the years due to excessive alcohol abuse. She was routinely seen inviting transient males to her residence for drinking and sex. She continued to live in the residence after a fire had nearly gutted the entire house....

I would read those words and tell myself, this woman was my mother. And then, the more uncomfortable thought, is my mother still.

* * *

When I was in Los Angeles to talk to the detective, I filled the hours of waiting for him by driving around town. Because I didn't want to go back to the house and face my father, because I didn't know where else to go, because Los Angeles is such a difficult place to navigate, I went to the only places that were familiar to me. I drove to each of the neighborhoods where I used to live, go to school, wander the concrete sidewalks and the canyons where fragrant eucalyptus and poisonous oleander clung to the slippery, decomposing granite hillsides, where the child I once was walked endlessly in the hours between the end of the school day and darkness.

After wending my way down from my father's home in Laurel Canyon, I went to find the first house I remembered living in as a child, on the corner of Fairfax and Sunset. It had been torn down and was now an apartment house. I drove by the next house I lived in, a few blocks up the hill, and found its façade had been so completely altered that it was unrecognizable. Even more confusing, the house had also been expanded into the empty lot next door, where as children we could kill an entire Saturday sliding down the slippery granite hillsides on pieces of cardboard, ending the day covered in a haze of dirt that crept into every crease and crevice of our skin. Although the houses were gone, the neighborhoods themselves had not changed substantially. I went to my grammar school and saw that the "temporary" classroom bungalows that had taken up so much of the school's playground space were still there. I walked through a park my grade school friends and I used to frequent, but the sight of a homeless person curled up under some shrubbery drove me away, jittery and fearful as I was. Everywhere I went I saw young men in street wear, sometimes gang wear, hanging out on corners, leaning against warehouse buildings, watching the world go by, looking for something, anything that might spur them to action. Sometimes there were girls draped on their arms or crouched at their feet, pulling on cigarettes or absently pushing baby strollers back and forth, over and over, in the same small square of space.

I could have ended up as one of those girls, I thought.

I drove to my junior high school, which I remembered as a series of drab, disconnected buildings surrounding an expanse of asphalt that was our playground and, in a corner, marked by a series of stark benches, our cafeteria. Now, the entire block was encased in a wrapper of tall chain-link fencing and gates relieved only by several large, angry signs that read, "Weapons not allowed on campus. If you bring firearms or other weaponry into school, you will be arrested or expelled." The children who attended this school would be only twelve, thirteen, fourteen years old.

I remembered walking to this school in the calm, cool mornings, putting on my usual air of casual alertness, eyes looking only forward, striding with purpose but not attitude, a stance designed to get me ignored instead of noticed, especially by the tough Chicano girls who leaned up against the warehouses outside school, smoking cigarettes, waiting for the first bell to ring.

Being noticed was dangerous. One of the many lessons I had learned from living with my mother.

As I sat there then, staring out my car window more than twenty years after the twelve-year-old girl I had been walked these same streets, a young man swaggering up the block yelled something to me. I couldn't tell if it was suggestive or provocative, intended to be inviting or intimidating. His smile could have been a challenge or a come-on. I rolled up the windows and locked the doors. I was surprised at how frightened I was. It was a feeling so unusual to the adult life I had made for myself, a feeling so long missing from my regular repertoire of emotions, that it took me a long, slow moment to remember that this feeling had been a constant companion of my childhood.

I turned the ignition, put the car in gear, and as I did, an exhortation came rising up from somewhere inside me I did not know existed. It said, "You belong here. Not in that farmhouse three thousand miles away, not at those polite dinner parties, not with a briefcase over your shoulder and shuffling along in a straight skirt, but here. Right here."

The voice startled me with its intensity. It was the voice of the girl I had been. She stared out at me from my past, her face a mask of pain habitually held in check. I thought I had been creating a new life, a safe life that fulfilled the dreams of the child I had been. In that moment, in her calling to me, I realized that the life I had made was beautiful, yes, but sometimes it was like wearing someone else's clothing. There was something about the fabric, the texture, that rubbed wrong, something about the fit that chafed and constricted.

I wanted to believe I'd left it all behind. I wanted the child I had been to do the same. But she was warning me that much of this old life was still within me and could not be simply discarded.

I had come back to Los Angeles to say good-bye to my father, to try to bury my mother. This girl I had been was asking me not to let her go in the process. She was warning me that I couldn't just bury the ugly parts of my past without also burying what might be the most important parts of myself.

$\mathscr{P}$hotographs

A few weeks after my mother's death, in the damp days at the end of November, I arrived in Los Angeles. I had already planned to spend Thanksgiving at my father and stepmother's house. When I got there, I asked about the house on Hudson Avenue with some idea of going over and seeing it—or what was left of it. What I hoped to find, I did not know. I had lived apart from her for almost a decade. Perhaps I just wanted some firsthand evidence of how she was living when she died. But my brother and father told me there was no point; they'd gone through it already and removed anything of value, mostly just paintings and photos. They made it clear, more by the looks on their faces than anything they said, that there was nothing I'd want to see. Or, perhaps, nothing they wanted to show me. My father shook his head and sputtered a few incomplete sentences about the state of the house, the damage, the soot, the mess. I imagined them wandering in its dark corners, among the litter, and didn't know whether I'd been cheated or spared something.

One unusually gray day after the holiday, I went out to my father's garage, where he said anything I might want had been stored. There were some paintings stacked against a wall. I pulled them apart and looked at the once familiar images, one by one: bold patches of chalky colors rendered a group of surfers, their bodies the color of bricks, clad in turquoise swim trunks, with acid yellow, seafoam green, and coral colored surfboards, flat against an imagined landscape of green hills and a magenta sky. On another canvas, a younger version of my mother stared out from a painting, a girl in a yellow dress, her hair hanging in plain black to her shoulders, her eyes saucers in her face. A different painting showed a man with a bouquet of roses, everything exploded and contained in squares and triangles of mauves, blues, peaches, pinks, and white.

I remembered these paintings from our house on Fairfax Avenue, the house where my earliest memories were made. I was amazed and relieved that so many of them had survived my mother's chaotic and dissipated life. These paintings and others had adorned the deep, early-evening blue walls of our expansive living room, which had a sunroom at one end and an arched picture window at the other. Sometimes my mother hung one of her creations in this window—a gossamer dress illuminated by the sunshine, its wide sleeves and flowing hem held aloft with fishing line tacked to the walls and ceiling.

Other times, there might have been a bedraggled Christmas tree there, months and months out of season, its needles dry and dropping onto the floor, silver icicles winking in the spring sunlight, half the bulbs dead and the other half blinking off and on to some aberrant rhythm. There was an upright piano in the far corner of the room, its dark wood stained in places by cigarettes that had been left to burn on the edge when an ashtray was not handy, or a glass had been left to sweat and weep a gray ring onto the finish, or a candle had never been blown out, leaving a small black wick afloat in a pool of soft, crayon-colored wax. There was always a guitar against the fireplace, with a missing string and cigarette burns in the neck from where people stuffed their butts while they played. There was a blue and maroon Oriental rug with tattered fringe and scattered stains where a dog or cat had barfed or taken a crap, a lit cigarette had fallen, or a wine glass had overturned.

My mother had made several oversize pillows, covered them in violet, navy, and magenta tie-dyed velvet, and tied long tassels to each corner. These cushions were strewn across the floor and served as impromptu mattresses for people who couldn't be bothered to drag themselves home or even as far as the pale blue sofa with the carved back and claw-feet, one of which had been broken when a body heavy with drink had fallen into it. The claw-foot had been nailed back in place, but it didn't always hold, and sometimes, when one of my mother's friends sat down too suddenly, the sofa jerked and tipped, sending the person's arms up in the air, cigarette ash sprinkling down, and wine splashing over the edge of a glass, while laughter erupted in the room and my mother yelled at my brother or me to go get some soda water and paper towels and wipe up the stain before it set. We ran, even though, or perhaps because, there were already so many other stains.

34

However, in the afternoon, during those precious, empty hours on the weekends of my childhood when we had cleaned up from the party of the night before but the party of the night to come had not yet begun, when the room was quiet and free of people, when the ashtrays were emptied, the glasses picked up, and the light streaming through the window was low enough to dissipate its native glare, then the room I usually avoided seemed safe enough for me to enter, to linger.

These paintings, now displaced in my father's garage, had drawn me in. They had covered the walls, so many of them in so many different shapes and sizes, outlined in plain blond or black wood, or ornate, almost baroque frames, placed just inches from one another. There were other paintings I remembered that were not in that garage. There was the compact, square block with a midnight and light blue checkerboard border set within another yellow and white checkerboard border that, in turn, surrounded a center square painted with an apple green heart. An ample canvas with five or six people lined up in a disorderly row, one painted in bold black strokes, another in watercolor, then oils, and onto charcoal pencil, a progression of different styles, of different artists, had hung high on a wall. One sheet of paper, suspended in a blond frame, was decorated with nothing more than a collection of black squiggling lines. Another larger sheet contained an assemblage of smears in ocher, khaki, and brown, fragmented by strokes of black. And there was that plaster piece of white wedding cake, complete with a pile of icing roses on top, which used to sit, inert and inedible, on a corner table.

I remembered, as a child, staring at these paintings because I wanted to extricate the stories they had to tell. I wanted to know why squiggly lines and smudges of color got the dignity of framing and hanging on a wall. I wanted to understand how a stroke of a pen made a person's expression seem not just real but inevitable. I wanted to find the images and associations buried in a pile of paint. I wanted to know why a magenta sky didn't seem strange. But more than all of that, I wanted the stories that each painting had to tell about my mother.

If I heard her coming down the stairs, no longer hungover, but her eyes sparkling, her mouth eager, her expression refreshed by an afternoon bath, her slept-in and smudged mascara, eye shadow, and lipstick now reapplied with the precision she learned as a model, I would position myself in the room in the hopes that she would see me there, and instead of turning toward the kitchen to pour her first glass of wine for the day, a benevolence of mood might turn her toward the living room, toward me, and she would tell me the stories that I had already heard but wanted to hear again.

"That painting, the one of all the different people, we did that one at a party," she'd say. "Someone started it, and people came by and added to it over the entire evening. Artist one minute, subject the next.

"The surfers…that was done by my old boyfriend, John Altoon. We went to art school together. He was my first love. They aren't signed because he threw all his work away. I took them out of the garbage can. He was furious when he found out and wanted to destroy them. I couldn't marry him…he was too crazy. And my parents hated him. I broke his heart. He's dead now."

Her voice so flippant, so matter-of-fact about these memories, this heartbreak.

"The wedding cake was a party favor a friend did. They gave them away to the guests," she'd continue. "See underneath? That silver scrawl? That's his signature. It says Claes Oldenburg. Craig Kauffman did that piece. That square one with the green heart is by Billy Al Bengston. The last show we went to at the Ferus Gallery had his work. That's Ed Ruscha. He did that book of all the photos of the Sunset Strip. That one you're always playing with, in the silver box that folds out a million times? Ed Kienholz did that one. He did that Barney's Beanery sculpture."

As if these names should mean anything to me. These artists, like so many of her friends, weren't famous yet. They were just people who hung out in paint-spattered pants. But they were on their way. Her voice said she knew it; everyone knew it. But what about her? I would wonder. Where was she on her way to?

* * *

At twenty years old, standing in my father's garage, I finally knew the answer to that question. I let the paintings fall back into place against the garage wall. As I did so, I knew I wanted one or two, maybe three, to take back home with me. I wanted to be reminded of the few good things that were leftover from her life. The only other artifacts my father had collected were contained in three or four enormous moving boxes scattered around, the tops opened like so many tongues. They were filled with photographs. Piles of them, barely contained by the cardboard, scraps of faces from every part of her life and many parts of mine, stared up in fragments of moments laughing, smiling, posing, overlapping, and spilling over one another, like insects foaming in a carcass. Sepia-toned images of my grandfather as a young man were mixed in with color snaps of my mother cavorting at a party. Baby pictures of my brother and me rubbed alongside photos of my mother and older half brother in Italy when he was just a toddler. I found pictures of her modeling in what looked like a European courtyard, and others of her passed out on a sofa, her face lax with drink-induced sleep. There were innumerable pictures of my brother when he was a laughing, chubby, towheaded boy. In almost every picture of me, I am serious, usually with my head cocked down and away, a finger or thumb against my lips, thinking, thinking, thinking. It's a position, a stance, I carried into adulthood. Again, I was flooded with relief that so many of these slices of life and time had somehow been preserved.

Different versions of many of these pictures had also adorned the walls of the house on Fairfax, and they had their own stories to tell. In one, my mother was standing on a pedestal, her hair cropped close to her head in black spikes that fell across her forehead and cheeks. She was wearing a one-piece bathing suit and pumps, people on either side of her holding out flowers and a long drape of gauzy fabric, their faces adoring, admiring, supplicating. I remembered her telling us that this was a photo still from a movie she appeared in. The film was on late-night television once, and we had to all stay up and watch through the entire boring movie, waiting, waiting for the one scene where she walked in, stood on the pedestal, arranged her legs just so, and then walked offstage.

That was it? I remembered thinking. That's all?

"See," she'd said. "I got that part after I won the Miss Redondo Beach contest. When I was modeling, just before I started at art school."

As if any of that would be meaningful to any of us.

In another photo, she was wearing a full skirt and bustier, a glass of champagne in one hand, a string of pearls wrapped around the other wrist. The chairs from our living room were in the background, but in the photo, the silk seats still gleamed, intact, unripped.

"That was when I lived in New York," she'd told me. "After I'd won that fashion design contest that got me my first job designing blouses. I had nothing to wear to a party, so I made the skirt and added beads to the top that same afternoon. I was dating Marlon Brando then. He was just starting out filming *On the Waterfront* across the river in Hoboken, New Jersey. But then I wrote an article about going out with him for *Glamour* magazine, and he stopped speaking to me. He hated publicity."

Dating a famous movie star? Even as a child, I was skeptical. Maybe she'd just met him once or twice. After all, she didn't seem to know any movie stars anymore. Or maybe it was true, but like so many other people, he had moved on, out of her life, after she did something to make him angry.

There was a picture of her squatting on the ground in a plaza, her arms outstretched, her hands open, a cluster of pigeons at her feet and perched on her shoulders. My half brother, six years older than I, to whom I'd not spoken in years, was an adorable, curly headed, dark little boy in this picture, clinging to our mother, his face screwed up in frightened tears.

"That was when I took Owen to Italy," I remembered her telling me. "Everyone told me I was crazy to bring such a young child to Europe. But he was so sweet back then. We had a wonderful time. Until my mother showed up. That bitch. Always following me and trying to horn in on my fun since she doesn't know how to have any herself. She only knows how to count money."

I stared at these photos and, just as I had as a child, tried again to reconcile the woman they depicted with the woman I had known. The photos showed a woman who was slender, elegant, stylish, won contests, had good jobs, dated famous men, looked out at the world—or at least into the camera—with an expression that seemed to say she expected only another date, another party, another opportunity, another win.

But that was all before. Before the pricks who got her pregnant, left her, and never sent money, never helped out at all, never lived up to their responsibilities. Before her controlling mother and penny-pinching father refused to help her. Before the Jew bastards who ran the garment industry downtown stole her ideas and refused to pay her for her talent. Before she was saddled with a bunch of spoiled brats. Before me. Before the daughter who was a bore, a drag, a tomboy, a disappointment.

I dug deeper into the boxes.

I found a fuzzy, tea-colored image of a group of young girls sitting in a field. My grandmother and her four sisters. They had bows in their hair, and three of them were focused on the baby sister in their midst while one sat apart, more sullen, looking at the camera. All the girls were sitting in a meadow that must have been near her childhood home on a hardscrabble farm in southern Vermont, the one Grandma always talked about, the one she told me she hoped to return to someday but was frightened of the cold. I set this photo aside. I found another one of the same set of girls, now young women, standing in front of a farmhouse, with an older woman, their mother undoubtedly, being attended to in the middle of the picture. There was a note on the back in my grandmother's delicate handwriting: Fair Haven, Vermont, July 4, 1917. She would have been eighteen years old then. She always said she was glad she was born in 1899 because she was one year older than the year she lived in. I set these images aside.

I found one of just her, her hair neatly, softly swept away from her face, her well-defined features in profile as she read a book; another of her, arms outstretched, this time her hair hanging down, cascading over her shoulders all the way to her waist. Somehow, even though the image was black and white, I saw her hair as mahogany colored. In this one in particular, I also saw many echoes of my mother's face—the strong nose, the square jaw, the wide mouth.

There were a number of pictures of my grandfather as a young man: handsome, wearing a bow tie and white shirt, or a navy uniform, or a topcoat with his arm through my grandmother's arm. In one, he's fishing with friends, in another, singing with a group of men playing accordion and piano, and in still another, he's standing outside a barrack-like building, smiling, naked except for a cluster of leaves he's holding in front of his private parts. I hadn't known him as someone with a sense of humor, only as a serious older man, not particularly fond of children, angry and withholding with his daughter in whom he was clearly and regularly disappointed.

There was a picture of him holding a model airplane, which reminded me of the story most frequently told of him while he was alive and after his death: he was talented and visionary, designed the first all-metal aircraft, the Spartan Executive, in 1936, but never got the credit he deserved, was not appreciated, didn't know how to get along with his managers, his bosses.

I added these photographs to my pile. I had no idea what I intended to do with the personal little collection I was creating. But so much had been lost already. I didn't know what might become of these boxes. I was afraid I'd lose whatever family record was left. I didn't want to take too many more chances.

I found pictures of my mother as a baby, a little girl standing next to her big brother, a cat draped through her arms. In one, marked Tulsa, Oklahoma, 1932, she was holding a toy plane. In another, she was wearing a bathing suit and cap, her mother kneeling next to her, smiling, cheek pressed affectionately to cheek. A memory came flooding back of my grandfather showing me this picture and asking me who I thought it was. I must have been only five years old—he died when I was six—and I was confused. I thought the photo showed my mother and me, the resemblance was so vivid, so striking. But I knew it couldn't be. The photo looked old, I'd never owned a one-piece bathing suit, and my mother wasn't affectionate with me in that way. My grandfather had smiled and patted my head as he told me it was my mother and grandmother; my consternation had been just what he intended. Then I was even more confused; I'd never before seen any demonstration of affection between my mother and grandmother.

There were also pictures of my grandfather as an older man; in one dated 1963, the year of my birth, he's wearing nothing but a snug bathing suit and slippers, arms held Atlas-style over his head, flexing his firm and well-built body. Apparently, it wasn't just the women in the family who were vain.

The pictures of my mother as she grew into a teenager and young woman showed cascades of hair, a full mouth, a bit of a snaggletooth smile—I recalled her telling me she had had braces—and most surprising to me, some shyness and reticence in front of the camera. By the time she was in her twenties, in the mid-1950s, her hair was cropped short; and in every picture, even the most casual setting, she had perfected the turned shoulders, the one bent leg, the pulled-back arms and dipped chin of someone who has been coached on how to set herself up for a camera. Beyond the beauty captured on film, there waited a shadow of self-defensiveness, self-protection.

I found a few photos of her with a man who must have been her first husband. I'd never met him, but I put together the date stamp with the stories she told us children about the guy who married her knowing she was pregnant with another man's child, but because he was so in love with her, he didn't care. This pregnancy resulted in my half brother. The man who gave Owen his last name divorced my mother after just a couple of years and then died young. My mother always told us she didn't know who got her pregnant but thought it might have been a famous movie producer.

Owen began to appear in the photos as a swarthy-skinned, dark, curly haired baby, holding a *Reader's Digest* upside down, wearing a white hat and sailor outfit coming off a plane, holding my mother's hand, or clutched in her arms as she stared at him adoringly. She had always said he was the most beautiful, the best baby, her voice tilted toward disappointment at the young man he turned out to be. I was astonished at the look on her face as she gazed at him, having seen so little pass between them that wasn't an argument or a screaming match.

I discovered a picture of my mother and father on what, judging by her simple white dress, a bouquet of roses in her hand, a sharp grin on my father's face, must have been their wedding day—another marriage necessitated by a pregnancy. My father was only in his early twenties, eight years younger than she was, and in the few pictures I find of their few years together as husband and wife, he is at that impossibly trim, handsome, hopeful, confident age of life. Another side of another parent that I had never witnessed myself.

I put aside the pictures of her as a bride. Evidence: these tiny snapshots were more evidence, of an earlier life and a side of my mother that I never knew.

My brother Jason in his baby pictures, which were the most numerous by far of any photographic subject matter, was a perfect, blond, chubby-cheeked cherub. In the pictures I found of myself, I am no different, other than my more taciturn expression. In fact, we were only a year and a half apart in age and as babies looked so much alike that people frequently asked if we were twins. My mother referred to us as the "Campbell's Soup Kids" after the pair who appeared on the labels. She also told me, frequently, that my brother had taken up so much of her attention that she never paid any attention to me as a baby and only visited me at night when I was sleeping in my crib.

I came to an image of myself as a diapered baby in my father's lap, he in a sling chair at the beach, a nipple-topped bottle in hand, my face pressing against his lips, his face obscured by a floppy orange hat. The party pictured was an annual July Fourth event, but by the time I had any memories of our attendance, my parents had been divorced for several years, my father had moved to New York, and the inherent innocence and joy the event in the photograph depicted had been stripped away, leaving not much more than a desperate clinging to times already passed. I found a photograph of the three of us children scrubbed and dressed up on my father's parent's sailboat and at the Sausalito Yacht Club.

Then Owen began to drop from the photographic record. It became just Jason and me, dirty, barefoot, with oddly chopped hair, in the scruffy back- or front yard of our sprawling, seen-better-times house at 1517 North Fairfax Avenue, the numbers painted pink next to the dark front door.

I found some pictures we must have sent home from a visit to our father, the woman who would become my stepmother, and her son, by now living in the first of their old farmhouses in New Jersey. Here, Jason and I were wearing overalls, riding ponies, pumping our legs on a rope swing, showing off the baskets of vegetables we helped grow in their extensive garden.

I plowed through countless images of my mother. Her once taut stomach became a pillow hanging over her bikini bottom. Her body thickened, her face reddened. Her smile was almost always the same, her full mouth opening on a row of straight, white teeth, her whole face brightening with the act. But strain started to appear in tightness about the lips and eyes, a feral nervousness in her expression. Some photos of her were simply unattractive, but a few were much worse, exposing her in various states of drunkenness, undress, passed out. I carefully set aside a few images from her last years that showed her in the best light possible, given the circumstances of her life.

There were two photographs from the last years of her life at the Hudson house. In one, she's sitting in a chair in the garden next door, her face alight with the simple surprise of someone pointing a camera at her. She looks worn, but not drunk, not degraded. In another, she is in a peach-tiled bathroom. A red-and-white striped dress hangs from her shoulders, over her distended stomach. She's looking back over her shoulder, toward the camera, making an effort to adopt a once-familiar modeling pose. But her hair is badly cut, her jawline no longer firm, her expression haunted. Her smile is not a record of feeling so much as a record of what she could do with her face. This picture was taken, I thought, within a year or so of her death.

I took the selected photographs home with me, back across the country. In a ritual act, I purchased an old-fashioned album with heavy pages the color of milky tea and a box of black photo corners. I organized the pictures chronologically and carefully licked the sour backs of the paper triangles, stuck them to the pages, and fit the photos into them; if I knew dates and names or found them scribbled on the back of a photo, I used my best handwriting to create a caption with this information. I started with the picture of my grandmother and her sisters in the field. I ended with the one of my mother posing in the peach bathroom.

When I was finished, I didn't really know what I had done or what I felt. I suspect I was trying, somehow, to create a coherent storyline to my mother's family history. To *my* family history. I thought there would be some satisfaction in that. But there was not as much as I had hoped. I had thought looking into my family's past, collecting the players in one place so I could give them my consideration and regard, would complete something for me, perhaps literally and figuratively close the book on those years gone by and thereby make my future as clean and fresh as a blank sheet of paper. It didn't work. At least not right away. I thought I might give it time.

But scanning through the pages over the years, considering the stories the images suggested, I did not feel the much sought-after "closure" people speak of. Even worse, I felt almost no connectivity to the images there. I tried adding happier, more recent photos of my life: my brother and me at his college graduation, a group of us at a gathering of my father's family in San Francisco, pictures of my father's second old farmhouse in New Jersey. These didn't help either.

From time to time, as the album moved with me from house to apartment, from apartment to house, I might leave the book out on a coffee table in the living room, an almost unconscious provocation—or perhaps, more simply, a hope—that a visitor, a friend, or a guest might ask, "What's this?" and hazard opening the pages. I rarely volunteered information about my mother and her family to anyone I knew. All of it seemed too complex, loaded, and fraught with difficulty to share in any social or polite context. And even if someone did pick up the book and turn the pages, marveling at the beauty of the images, the beauty of some of the people depicted, and the history suggested therein, I hesitated to offer anything but the most basic information. And when I did, I spiced it up from time to time with one of the perhaps apocryphal stories about my grandfather's work as an aircraft engineer, my mother's dates with Marlon Brando, the time I allegedly fell off a table and cracked my skull as a baby.

I didn't know how to square any of these little anecdotes with all that I knew was behind the photos, with the reality I carried with me, and didn't know how to share, if I could or should share, if it even mattered. Everyone I encountered had a kind of shorthand about their childhoods, their parenting. This shorthand assumed so many things about the expected commonalities among childhoods. So many stories began with phrases like "You know, when you were a kid and your parents piled you all in the station wagon and...." To which I would nod politely or say something dismissive and vague, like, "Well, my childhood was a little different, but please, do go on." I wanted the album to do what I could not, to offer a pleasant shortcut through the ages.

One day, maybe a decade after I made the album, a good friend, someone with whom I had spent enough long hours to share some stories about my mother and even stories about the child I had been—I was, after all was said and done, even more reluctant to talk about myself than about my mother—came upon the album and began to look through it. For her, the pictures conjured little news. They were depictions of people and events with which she already had passing familiarity. Her questions were more about connecting the dots between what she'd already heard from me and what she was seeing in the photos. Being a careful, thorough person, she turned each page slowly, regarded each image completely, and did not stop her progression until she reached the blank pages at the end. Then she closed the book, placed it back on the antique child's wagon I had repurposed as a coffee table, and said, "That wasn't as bad as I expected."

I said, obviously enough, that I had made a highly edited selection and not included the uglier images.

"Of course," she said.

We moved on to other topics, but the comment stuck with me. It wasn't that I wished I had made a more tragic picture. It was simply that I had, knowingly, consciously, made an incomplete picture and had maintained a vague hope that this simulacrum would do. It wasn't that I wanted to linger on the degraded parts of my mother's life; I had already lived through plenty of it alongside her. It was that I wanted to do a better job of trying to understand how the darker parts had come to be. How had the girl with the idyllic childhood steeped in the optimism and opportunity of Southern California in the forties and fifties—model, artist, fashion designer, friend of famous artists, models, and actors—become a drunken, sodden, street person who was stabbed and strangled in a burned-out building, her clothes ragged, her ancient, one-eyed, short-legged little dog standing over her, growling at the police who came to the scene?

Then, the question even stranger to me, how had I come out of my childhood with so few visible scars?

I realized that my entire relationship with my mother had been defined, by both of us, by all the ways I was different from her. She was a free spirit, self-indulgent, fun; and I was diligent, bookish, boring. She was city and I was country; she, West Coast and I, East Coast. Our lives seemed to represent two neatly opposing arcs: she'd been given every advantage as a child and made a mess of things; I'd been neglected, taunted, exposed to inappropriate behavior, and yet I came through as strong, independent, successful.

It began to occur to me that our stories could be more interesting than all that. I began to want my mother's life to be more than just a Hollywood tragedy; I began to want my life to be something more than simply an antidote to hers.

Fairfax

Our house on Fairfax Avenue was a sprawling, gray, stucco-covered behemoth with a red-tiled roof. This is where my mother, brother, half brother, and I lived through the late sixties and early seventies, from when I was three or four to eight or nine years old, in the closest semblance to a family that we ever had. The house had a heavy, chocolate-colored, arched, wooden front door that opened into an adobe-tiled foyer where visitors could wait and watch and admire my mother as she descended the open staircase, her long fingers lightly sliding down the wrought-iron railing, her hips swaying as she crossed her shapely legs one in front of the other, head held aloft, shoulders stretched down and back.

To the left of the foyer was a dining room with a wall of windows looking out over the front porch, which was surrounded by a low wall that stepped down to a front yard and concrete walk that led out to a sidewalk. At the end of the hall was a room with a curved wall of leaded glass windows that cranked open onto a bed of rosebushes. Two heavy sewing machines that looked to me like miniatures of the oil rigs I saw on the drive to my grandmother's house had been pushed up against the windows. My mother called it the breakfast room, even though it was never used until the sun was well up into the afternoon or had already set for the evening. There were some glass-fronted cabinets in which my mother kept mismatched and chipped china plates and a few faceted wine glasses. There was a round table, scarred and stained by spilled wine and cigarette burns, which my mother covered in a floor-length cloth of brilliant yellow, orange, and pink flowers with purple pom-pom trim. She and her friends often sat at this table through the afternoon and into the evening, eating an improvised meal of grapes, crackers, smelly cheeses, cold bright shrimp, and a can of smoked oysters stuck with toothpicks.

Sometimes my brother and I, but more often just I, would crawl among the tangle of human and chair legs and sit in the floral tent the tablecloth made, listening to the rise and fall of adult voices, trying to match each person to the rise and fall of their emotions as they spoke of the bastards in power, politics, and the garment industry; who was making it in the art world and who'd been screwed; who was getting it on and who was moving out; who had had a bad trip and who was getting their act together.

This room led to a white-tiled kitchen with white painted cabinets and a beige linoleum table and then to a narrow laundry room that, in turn, led to a shadowy space at the back of the house where only a few high windows let in any light. The maid's room, my mother called it. This was where, from time to time, one of the Mexican women who was simultaneously baby-sitter, pattern maker, and seamstress might live, putting her few belongings into the wide closet along one wall and the drawers in the peach-tiled bathroom. Many of these women came and went, but in my memory, they all blended into a single woman with caramel-colored skin and black coffee eyes who would sit with me after kindergarten while I ate my bowl of Campbell's chicken noodle soup. As I slurped noodles from my spoon, she would point to things, giving me their Spanish names, showing me how to form my lips around the unfamiliar words and string them into sentences that sent her mouth into a smile and her hands to her lips to cover her crooked and tarnished teeth.

But these women never stayed long, suddenly packing their things into crumpled shopping bags as my mother screamed at them for some imagined insult or accused them of stealing some object that eventually turned out to have been misplaced, lost, or borrowed. They fled out the side door, muttering in Spanish, and then waited at the end of the driveway for a beat-up sedan to arrive with a cousin or a brother behind the wheel; and although I didn't understand everything they said, I knew it had something to do with a bad mother who drank too much and didn't take care of her beautiful children.

The same door that expelled the Mexican woman also led to a large expanse of sandy soil patched with grass and several singular trees and shrubs. An enormous and ancient avocado tree dropped fruits that my brother and I sold for a nickel apiece at an improvised stand on the sidewalk out front. A persimmon tree shed mushy orange globs, which squished up between our toes as we chased each other, barefoot, through the yard; sometimes my mother peeled and ate one, disgusting us with a dribble of orange phlegm dripping from the corner of her mouth, down her chin. There was a shrub with small, glossy leaves that had once been trimmed into a circle, with a dead patch in the center where my brother, his friend Kenny, and I would play "I'll show you mine if you show me yours." There was a rock-edged pond with malfunctioning plumbing that left it habitually dry other than the few times we dragged a hose to the top of the waterfall, where it cascaded down the rocks until our mother yelled at us to turn it off because we were running up the water bill.

At the far end of the yard, we could reenter the house through the sunroom. A narrow room, with a tiled floor and walls of windows, where my mother kept an easel and art supplies, a chaise where she would ask a friend or one of us to lie down and provide her with a model. If there was no one around, a sleeping cat or dog or the flowering birds of paradise outside the windows would do. She also kept an old wicker baby carriage in this room. It was lined with red felt cushions and piled with dolls she had kept from her childhood.

"Why did I have a daughter who won't play with dolls?" she asked me over and over. "What's wrong with you that you won't play with dolls? I saved them for you, for the baby doll daughter I always wanted, and now you won't play with them. You won't play with any dolls at all."

I was guilty as charged. I could never figure out just how someone was supposed to play with dolls, never knew what it was one was supposed to do with them. And I disliked her dolls especially. I hated their overt femininity, stiff black lashes, hard porcelain heads, glass eyes that seemed to follow me in judgment and condemnation every time I passed. The heart-shaped lips and wide-open eyes of these dolls were reflected in almost every drawing or watercolor my mother ever made, an ongoing rebuke to my ongoing disinterest.

This sunroom led through a wide opening into the living room, the room with all the paintings and photographs on the walls. This was also the room where the party often began or ended. Throughout the hours of the afternoon and into the early evening, the phone would start to ring, and the doors of the house would open and shut or just stay open, voices would jumble together in greeting, and the gathering would begin. People came and went but mostly came, brown bags tucked under their arms from which they would liberate some booze, a few packs of cigarettes, maybe some food they'd picked up at the gourmet market that had just opened on the opposite corner of Sunset and Fairfax. They also brought instruments, artwork, and stories. They sat around and played and talked and smoked and drank and sketched one another playing and talking and smoking and drinking. Jason, even as a child of only five or six, could always be relied upon to entertain the adults with an amusing story or anecdote about something that had happened at school or at our house during some other gathering.

"Jason, darling, you're so funny, you're so charming," my mother would say, wrapping her arm around his waist, tugging him into the curve of her body. "Tell us about the time when...."

Owen's friends also stopped by, mingled in, joined the party as wannabe adults, changed records to keep the music constant and loud, fetched wine, drank what was left in a glass or directly from the bottle in the kitchen, bummed cigarettes, took drags on joints before passing them along. They played poker and won money from the disinterested or inebriated adults. By the time Owen was a teenager, his girlfriend, Melinda, sometimes spent the night. She had heavy eyebrows and sensuous, honey-colored hair that hung to her waist in loose waves, all things I coveted; she also had a soft voice and a gentle manner, bending her legs to meet me eye-to-eye when she stopped to ask me some question, engage me in brief conversation, all things I craved.

Because the unfettered energy of these parties unnerved me and I had no desire or idea how to participate in all the uninhibited expression of the late 1960s "letting it all hang out" ethos, I wandered the edges of the gathering like someone waiting for an accident to happen. I draped myself in a doorway, curled into a chair in a corner, sat cross-legged under a table, or just stood, limp against a counter, watching, waiting, and hoping for a general sputtering out as resources dwindled rather than a full-speed crash.

People would sit around the kitchen table or along the bus stop bench that had somehow arrived in our backyard along with a random collection of chairs and a picnic table that was beginning to pull apart; but most often, they scattered themselves among the pillows, sofas, and instruments in the living room. An accretion of glasses, ashtrays, beer cans, wine bottles, pads of paper, felt-tip pens, charcoal pencils, jugs of gray water, tin cans filled with brushes, and palettes filled with smudges of watercolors grew on whatever surface was nearby. A guitar or two, harmonicas, bongo drums, and sometimes something more exotic, like a sitar, lay in laps, at feet, or on an empty chair. Hands and arms were in constant motion, jogging and dancing across a pad of paper, reaching to fill a glass, wrapping around another person's shoulder or waist, strumming a guitar, pushing a harmonica against lips, shaking a cigarette up out of a pack, lighting a match.

When the hands moving across the page were my mother's, the tempo was staccato, a burst of sure, graceful strokes that inexplicably captured the slope and weight of someone slouching into the corner of a sofa or hanging over a guitar or holding a drink aloft. She always made a person's eyes a little larger, the lips a little fuller, the face a tad more glamorous then they were in real life. And in this, she always made the person look a little like her. She never finished the hands. With a swoop of the brush, she left just the suggestion of fingers. She couldn't be bothered with details, she said. She left these things for other people. I was disappointed by her lack of patience but even more by the way she covered it up. I loved her work, but I hated her excuses.

The gatherings of my mother and her friends also took place at other locations, and we children always went along. If it was a Saturday evening and an opening was scheduled, the party would be at an art gallery down on La Cienega—a plain building with a plain sign printed with a single word in simple serif type over its window: *Ferus*. The gallery doors opened onto a large, blank space of blond floors and white walls where adults wandered with small plastic cups of white wine or stood, an elbow cupped in the palm of an opposite hand, and discussed whatever it was hanging on the walls or displayed on white pedestals strategically placed throughout the room. I saw it all through a scattered forest of adult legs clad in fishnet stockings or white go-go boots, slick pants with flared-out legs, or simply skin that disappeared into the faraway hem of a miniskirt. I had to tilt my head backward to consider the art on the walls, and as I did, I listened to the words that drifted down from the adults, their discussions of meaning and artist intention, the use of white space, and something called "irony."

I looked at the colors, forms, and empty spaces; and when, on the rare occasion I was noticed and asked what I thought, I answered carefully. I described the animals I saw masked in abstract shapes on the canvas, or the feelings the colors brought to mind, or why the arrangement of the subject in that piece over there made it my favorite. My observations were always met with a nod, a smile, a look of surprised acknowledgement that passed between the adults, sometimes a small chuckle. Art was obviously important, but having an opinion about it seemed even more important.

Once all the wine had been drunk and the trays of food held only a few widely dispersed grapes, some skeletal-looking stems, a rind of cheese, a handful of pale crackers, anyone still left at the gallery would depart, only to reconvene at Barney's Beanery, where the same people from the gallery were now slung along the bar or around the picnic tables in the open dining room.

Plates of food, glasses of wine, and mugs of beer would appear; and everyone would share whatever was at hand, sipping one another's drinks, dipping spoons into one another's bowls of chili, taking bites from another person's burrito, stuffing morsels into the open mouths of wandering children as if they were fledgling birds. I wove myself in and out and around my mother's legs and the barstools, clinging to her, asking, when I got a glimpse of her attention, when we were going home. My voice was usually drowned out by the din of adult conversation, the laughter, and "witty repartee," as my mother called it. If I whined or squirmed too much, she might snap at me to go sit down somewhere, to stop bothering her, to quit trying to ruin her fun. To go "play." Which the other kids running around seemed able to do.

My mother's boyfriend, Henry, might bring me up into his lap or take me over to a table where there was food. Henry had wavy, chestnut-colored hair, eyes that crinkled at the corners, lips that were large and pillowy, and a prominent nose already going red with drink. He lived with us—and loved us—for a couple of years from when I was perhaps six to eight. Both he and my mother said he was a sculptor. I rarely saw him sculpt, and I don't remember him ever having a job. But he did make us a barbecue out of an old barrel and the legs of the now-broken swing set, welding a curly tail on one end and a pig's head on the other, along with a snout that could be turned to release smoke from two nostril holes. He'd sit with me for a minute or two and help me negotiate a sloppy burrito and tell me a story designed to bring a smile to my face. He inevitably got distracted by someone calling to him from across the room, or he'd need another drink, or my mother would want him to come corroborate a story, and I would be left folding and unfolding a napkin, pushing at the mess of beans and sour cream as I waited for the time when my mother would start to slur or cry or stumble or even, more than once, fall off her barstool, finally drunk enough that Henry would decide it was time to take us home and put her to bed.

From time to time, the gathering would be at a park where hundreds or maybe thousands of people collected for what was called, in the parlance of the time, a "love-in." When, in the middle of a weekend day, I saw my mother and Henry putting on headbands, digging up blankets, collecting musical instruments, and filling a white Styrofoam cooler with ice and beer, I, knowing what was forthcoming, would start to cry.

"Please, please, please, just leave me here," I would beg.

Shaking my head, twisting my body like a cat that doesn't want to be held, I would squirm in Henry's arms as he carried me to the car, accompanied by the litany of my mother's exasperated voice telling me to stop being such a drag. She said I was too young to leave at home. I thought I was too young to go to a love-in. There would be lots of other kids there, they said. Why couldn't I just relax and come along? My brothers and mother would start chanting a little song about me, the baby, the drag, the one who was no fun.

We would park behind a long line of cars and then trek up the road until we came to an open area where people swarmed across lawns already growing brown from foot traffic. There were people painting flowers and rainbows onto faces, plaiting beads and ribbons into hair, offering sticks of incense, a drink, a cigarette, a joint, or a few pills that promised to make you happier or mellower than you already were. There were people twirling and skipping in flowing, tie-dyed skirts and peasant blouses, or without shirts at all, their thin, bare chests or small, drooping breasts open to the air and sunshine. Music blasted outward from a stage so far away that the musicians seemed like miniature puppets, and then from the innumerable guitars, harmonicas, bongo drums, and tambourines that people everywhere played, clutching the instruments as if to keep afloat on the wash of humanity. Smiles were sloppy, eyes were glassy, and people fell into one another's arms or tangled together on a blanket or the lawn or in the mud, their mouths, limbs, and skin loose and open against one another.

We threaded our way among the crowd looking for an unoccupied space just large enough to accommodate our blanket and five bodies. Having been burned several times already, I was especially careful to avoid cigarettes held in outstretched hands made careless with drink or drugs. Once we had found a place to land, I stayed there, clinging to our thin raft set down among turbulent seas. I shook my head no when asked if I didn't want to come along and get my face painted or my hair braided. My brothers, mother, and Henry wandered the grounds and came back with stories of people making out, making music, having bad trips. I kept my head down and waited for it all to be over.

Sometimes the party was up in Malibu at a friend's long, low, glass-walled house where nudity was the norm and people gathered to swim, sauna, and climb the steep, dry hills with the owner's twenty or so almost identical, closely related, black dogs. At the end of the day, this artist and filmmaker would whistle together a writhing mass of sleek, dark animals near a large workbench where he kept cases of Kal Kan dog food. He emptied the large blue-and-white checkered cans into a dozen large bowls and then flattened the cans in a clamp bolted to the edge of the rough table. The cans were slowly being reused as shingles to make a shining, navy and silver roof on the studio he was building out back under the eucalyptus trees. The half-wild dogs swarmed about my legs as I stood by watching them merge into a mass of tumbling liquid; it was like trying to pet the sea.

Malibu was where Owen learned to drive. The ancient, topless jeep was jammed with several adults yelling directions and a fistful of kids clinging to the roll bars and screaming in fear as he careened the vehicle around the winding dirt roads sliced out of the steep hillsides, sending the vehicle up on two wheels on one corner, dropping a wheel off the edge on the next.

Malibu was where no one bothered with clothes but wandered from the hand-built pool to the hand-built sauna tacked onto the side of the hand-built studio, into the kitchen of the hand-built house to make a sandwich out of a hind of ham on the chopping block, and then back to a lounge chair, naked.

I was a reluctant nudist, sitting morose and uncomfortable at the edge of the pool while steaming flesh fled from the roasting sauna and plunged into the unheated, cerulean-blue pool. The filmmaker would swim over to me where I sat with my chin on my bent knees, his thinning hair plastered against the dome of his skull, his pale blue eyes puzzled and concerned.

"Don't you want to enjoy the pool?" he'd say. "Why don't you undress and swim? Come join us."

Of course, I wanted to swim. But I wanted to do it wearing the swimsuit my mother had refused to bring, saying no one else would be wearing one, so why should I? The filmmaker's voice was gentle, his entreaty sincere. My mother called out to him to leave me alone, that the attention only made me more stubborn. Faced with up to a dozen different naked children and adults, all apparently content, all happy, all comfortable, I couldn't articulate my inchoate feeling that all this multigenerational, multigender nudity was somehow, quite simply, wrong. I couldn't express my embarrassment at my mother's large breasts and pillowy stomach on display because she executed perfect dives and swam in long, elegant strokes from one end of the pool to the other, telling stories when she emerged from the water about her experiences as a synchronized swimmer and all the awards she'd won as a younger woman.

From time to time, I would be prevailed upon, I would decide to give it a try, or I'd simply give in to the disappointed, pleading looks. I would slowly undress, piling my clothes on a lounge chair strategically placed so I could keep my eyes on them because I had an irrational fear that they'd somehow disappear or be moved or hidden from me, and I'd be destined for perpetual nudity. Walking almost in a crouch, I'd enter the pool at the end with a set of steps, while people simultaneously smiled and tried not to watch, relieved and victorious that I had finally joined the party. Once in the water, I tended to stay there, even if that meant simply sitting on the steps, my arms clasped around my knees, covering my body as much as possible. Sometimes I'd venture into the pool, and the water rushing by all parts of me as I swam, unobstructed by a suit, felt decadent and, I had to admit, delicious.

Sometimes, when I found the effort to reconcile all these contradictory feelings and sensations too difficult, when I didn't want the sight of me to be an irritation to the others, I just stayed indoors. The living room had plenty of oversize books filled with art and photographs. There was a compact loft space tucked above the hallway, accessible by a ladder, with a mattress, comforter, and walls lined with books. I'd hide there, reading and dozing, waking from a shallow nap in the dim darkness to the sound of people saying, "Where's Lolly?" as they came in to refill their drinks or to nibble on the carcass of ham. I rarely answered, listening instead to their speculations that I was wandering around outside, that I was asleep in a bedroom, that, as usual, I was not participating, that I should be left alone.

A fate I was almost able to recognize, even then, as not unwelcome, as, in fact, exactly what I wanted.

If it were the Fourth of July, the party would extend over a long weekend at the beach in Santa Monica or Malibu, where people would set up multicolored tents in a long line along the white sand. Every night, fireworks displays would begin in the front of each tent, campfires and sparklers lighting up the beach, rockets and cascading clusters lighting the dark sky and reflecting off the even darker water, the show spreading half a mile or more up and down the beach. We had a muted green army surplus tent with a large flap for a door. Henry would set up a ring of stones for our campfire and cooking pot while I sat on the sand watching the fireworks and lighting the little black disks that grew suddenly into twisted snakes that then dissipated into nothing more than flecks of ash dispersed by the salty breeze. I twirled sparklers, staring into their shooting stars, and then collected the spent metal spikes from ours and others' campfires so I, or someone else, wouldn't step on them later, perhaps still hot, always sharp and painful against a foot.

After a few days, one by one, the other tents would be taken down, sand shaken from blankets, cars loaded with coolers and umbrellas. All except ours, now standing alone on the beach, empty of everything except dried-up seaweed, shells without their other halves, the occasional empty can of tuna or beer, a dropped sandal, a plastic bucket with a broken handle. The floor of our tent by now was littered. Damp clothes were jammed into corners, towels that would never fully dry hanging from the supports, blankets embedded with sand. Our faces were glazed with ocean water, our hair tangled with salt spray. My brothers and I would spend the days—which always seemed to turn perpetually gray and overcast once everyone else had left—wandering among the rocky outcroppings. We would crouch by the tide pools where we reached in with tentative fingers to touch the sticky anemones; prod small, scuttling crabs; and lift starfish to watch the rhythmic movement of their thousands of tiny feet. I found a turquoise and silver ring jammed between two rocks, which when freed almost fit my finger.

I met a young man with wavy brown hair that hung to his shoulders, who wore a leather and bead necklace he'd made from an animal he'd shot with an arrow and then ate while backpacking in some mountains. He sat at the tide pools with me, talking quietly with long intervals of silence, and for a time afterward, he wrote me letters on the backs of brown paper bags postmarked from places I'd never heard of. Once he sent me my own leather and beaded necklace he'd made from a different animal he'd shot.

Late in the afternoon, Henry and my mother would send my brothers and me off to collect mussels from the rocks. We would hold out the fronts of our T-shirts like aprons, adding the largest ones we could find onto our growing piles and returning to the tent laden with the night-sky-blue mollusks. Henry would put some ocean water and seaweed into our big, speckled, enamel pot and hold it out to each of us to dump our gleanings in. He'd sprinkle some wine over the mussels and set the pot on the fire to steam. Once the shells had popped open, we would cluster like crones around the cauldron, removing the hot mussels one by one, prying them open, gripping the rough beards between our teeth, and pulling them away with dirty fingers so the cooked mollusks dropped into our mouths. Strangers wandering by would yell or speak earnestly to us, warning us that mussels were poisonous at this time of year and we were going to die from eating them. My mother and Henry told us to ignore these people—how could anything natural be bad for us, they said—and because we were left with only a can or two of deviled ham and half a sleeve of saltine crackers, we did. Besides, the orange flesh was deliciously salty and sweet, and if you were lucky, like my mother always was, you might find a pearl, which you could clean with your tongue and then add to the collection growing in the bottom of a blue-freckled tin mug.

When everyone but us had been gone for days, when our tans were invisible under the salt that encrusted our skin, our hair so thick with sea air that we could no longer run our fingers through it, the food and booze had finally run out, and the largest mussels had been picked from the nearby rocks, Henry would drag everything out of the tent, pile it on a blanket, and tie the corners together. Then he would take down the tent as my mother sat in the detritus and cried, saying that she didn't want to go back to the dirty dishes, the house, the bills, the bastards downtown. She was a "Campfire Girl," she said, as if this explained everything. Henry wiped away her tears with his thumb and said that when they got back to the house, he was going to throw away all our keys and smash all the mirrors.

We would then pile everything into the trunk, perversely located in the front of the car; overloaded, the hatch would cant and twist, so Owen would have to push one side and Jason the other, while Henry secured the catch. The latches over the top of the windshield, frozen with salt spray, wouldn't accept the hasps on the convertible top, so stiffened from disuse that they no longer fully extended. We'd put on every piece of clothing we had brought, my mother would clamp a hat onto her head, my brothers would pile into the backseat, their feet on top of a cooler and the bundled-up tent, and I would crawl into the wooly compartment behind them. It was a space meant for storage, but it was just the right size for a skinny seven-year-old girl if I curled up on myself in the close, dark space, my arms wrapped around my body and my head tucked against my shoulder. Then we would take off amid the dense fog rolling in from the sea, Henry zipping the pale blue car along the twisting Pacific Coast road while my mother and brothers slept, their heads askew on their necks. I burrowed as deeply as I could into my small cave, turning my body in on itself, trying to avoid the damp air that lashed my sticky hair against my salt-rimed cheek.

* * *

On a few occasions, my father showed up at the house on Fairfax. According to my mother, our father was a bastard who abandoned her with his brats and never sent any money, never helped at all. In her worse insult of all, she said he was nobody until he met her—a child, a college boy. She said she had introduced him to everyone who was anyone, and then he left her. I suspected that my mother was right about my father. He wasn't around much. He didn't send her money. He simply said he didn't have any on those occasions when he came into the house to drop us off or pick us up. At the sight of him, she would begin screaming from the upstairs hallway, her voice bouncing and pinging off the high walls and ceilings of the foyer like a small, hard object that could leave us all with bruises.

I never questioned my parents' being apart because I'd never known them to be together. They divorced when I was an infant. He moved across the country when I was four. I also didn't blame my father much for his parental lapses because I knew how difficult my mother was to live with. Who would want to live with her if they had another choice? Who would want to give her money simply to watch her spend it on booze and cigarettes? I adored my father both in the blind way that young girls adore their daddies and because, when he did spend time with us, there was always a project to work on, a thing to be learned, an opportunity to play.

My dad might pick up my brothers and me on a hot Saturday afternoon and take us into Laurel Canyon to visit his friends who had a pool. Driving up the winding, eucalyptus-scented roads, he'd remind me that I was named after this place, point out the remnants of what had once been Houdini's castle, show us the short street with the tiny house hidden behind a fence where we had once all lived together, back in the time before I had memories.

Once he came over and set up a slightly unbalanced swing set, hurrying, trying to get it bolted together as my mother yelled at him in escalating volume. He ducked his chin and grinned sheepishly, apologizing to my brothers and me, telling me not to cry, not to worry, patting us on the heads as he scuttled away. I stood, kicking at the dirt, tears trickling down my face. Jason

stood beside me, laid his arm over my shoulders, and told me
he knew I missed Dad, but at least now that he was gone Mom
would stop screaming. Unlike me, Jason often managed a sense
of humor about our mother.

Sometimes Dad took us to an apartment he had in one of
the turrets that formed a corner of the building that housed the
merry-go-round at the Santa Monica Pier. I would sit at a round
table in the living room that looked out over the gray beach,
watch the waves break through the fog and crash into the sand
as the glittering sounds of the carousel music wafted upward, and
wish I could stay forever, that I didn't have to go home. He might
take us to the giant slide at the pier, where we trudged up a long
flight of stairs and were given a piece of burlap by a tanned teenage boy in long shorts with hair hanging around his face and in
his eyes. My brothers sat at the top and shot down the polished
metal to the bottom, each on his own square of gunnysack. I was
too small, too scared to go all alone, so I sat between my father's
legs and swallowed my breath like a hunk of ice as we whizzed
down the slick slide. I was glad to be too small, too scared; I was
glad to have an excuse to be so close to my father.

Then he moved to a small bungalow behind some unused
railroad tracks and a hot dog stand in a leafy section of West
Hollywood, where he grew snapdragons in his yard and dared
us to put our fingers in the flowers' throats. He had a drafting
table set up in a spare room of this house and showed us how to
make prints by carving shapes into potato halves, dipping them
in paint, and pressing them to sheets of white paper. A line of pale
blue deer ran across the page. Pink pigs collected beneath yellow stars on another. For lunch, he toasted small pieces of whole
wheat bread and stirred the fruit from the bottom of a yogurt
cup. I never told him that I preferred to dig down and uncover

the sweet, gooey fruit myself. I was too deeply impressed by these simple attentions, which were absent from my interactions with my mother.

Sometimes Dad would show up in the mornings to take Jason to his preschool at the top of Laurel Canyon, off Mulholland Drive. I was jealous that my brothers were going to school and I was not, had already spent time wailing over being left behind. I wanted a life beyond my mother's house, as it seemed my brothers had. I also didn't want to grant my brother the further privilege of all that extra time alone with our father. I begged to go along; my father pleaded with me to stay behind.

"You'll get carsick, just like you always do," he'd say. "You don't want to be vomiting on the drive home, do you?"

"Please, please, please," I'd say, tears dripping over my cheeks.

"I don't have time to bring you back," he'd say. "I have to get to work. I'll see you next weekend. I'll bring you next time."

I had nothing to negotiate with other than my raw and ragged desire to be with him. Sometimes, luck conspired with me. My brother had gotten up late and wasn't ready to go; my father didn't have the energy to argue; our mother was already yelling over the railing, clutching a robe at her throat. Her voice, thick with last night's drinking, screamed at him to just take me, the little, spoiled brat, just get me out of the house so she could have some peace and quiet. My father had neither the stomach nor the energy for confrontation, so he might give in just to avoid the noise, and I'd scramble into the car, accepting the backseat on the way there, knowing that I'd get the front seat on the way home. I'd stare out the window, and even though my father clenched his teeth and my brother slipped into sheepishness over being late again, I relished the physical sensations of relative peace and my small victory. I tried to enjoy these few small moments before the inevitable nausea crept up, pushing aside in its tumult all other feelings.

I'd watch the steep slopes of decomposing granite, scrubby oleander, and gracious eucalyptus rush by and try to fight down the waves that splashed and tumbled in my stomach every time the car took one of the innumerable turns on the winding canyon roads. My dad, in his rage at being enraged, was driving too fast. I'd hold my arms tight against my sides, swallow often, roll down the window when the bitterness began to rise at the back of my throat, and turn my face, like a dog, into the wind coming through the window. Sometimes I'd win. Sometimes, after my brother ran from the car, waving to us as he rushed to join the other children already lined up and almost all the way through the schoolhouse door, those moments as we came down the hill again would be uninterrupted by sickness. Sometimes I'd get to be just a little girl and her father, alone in the car together. In those moments, I'd feel vaguely embarrassed, simultaneously peaceful, and uncomfortable in solitude with this man I had no memory of living with, whom I felt I hardly knew and yet craved both because I wanted him and I wanted the escape he provided from my mother.

* * *

Someone to whom I once told a much-abbreviated version of the roughest outlines of my childhood experiences asked me a simple question: "Who took care of you?"

There were so many assumptions contained within that inquiry about the nature of relations between parents and children that I couldn't begin to answer her. My childhood didn't just contravene these perfectly acceptable ideas; these notions simply didn't apply to us.

While there were some adults around who offered a counterexample to our lifestyle—grandparents, schoolteachers, a few parents of friends—like most young children, we didn't question our upbringing, reckless as it was. My mother didn't think children needed to be taken care of, and her children seemed to agree. She often bragged to friends, "Oh, so many mothers bitch and complain about having to get up and make their kids lunch. I never get up, and the kids just make their own lunches." In my mother's circular reasoning, we were already so independent, she didn't need to be concerned for our welfare; of course, her indifferent parenting was exactly what made us so self-reliant. In truth, as much as we may have resented the cause or the source of this self-reliance, it was—and is—still a badge of honor we all carried with no small degree of diffident pride.

In fact, we were not exceptional. We were not the only children at the parties our mother brought us to. Yes, I had friends from more conventional homes, places where fathers worked and mothers kept up the house and made snacks for their children and their children's friends. But some of these parents knew my mother at least a little; they heard about the parties at our house and even sometimes attended. And although it was true that when children on the playground marveled that my mother "let" me make my own lunch of peanut butter and jelly on saltine crackers, I marveled that their mothers made them tidy sandwiches of cold cuts. Some even put slender slices of lemon into the plastic bags with the cut fruit so the apples wouldn't turn brown.

But it is also true that I coveted neither their lunches nor the parental attention they demonstrated. I loved my freedom and independence, regardless of the source or cause. I loved—and still love—more than anything, to be left alone.

As an adult, I discovered the writer Joan Didion. Through her essays, I was introduced to children in San Francisco who grew up about the same time I grew up in Los Angeles. These parents blew pot smoke into their children's faces or gave them acid on a regular basis. To keep their minds free and innocent. To keep them "turned on."

Well, I thought, at least my mother wasn't doing that. She didn't even like drugs.

The truth is that my mother was not unlike many parents of her era, her location, who didn't care very much what their children did as long as they didn't keep the adults from doing what they wanted to do. Among her crowd, children were not seen as domesticated pets that needed coddling, grooming, encouragement of their self-esteem, or even much attending to at all. This dismissiveness was a choice—conveniently self-serving, certainly, as are most choices—as ideal parenting was considered to be leaving children alone to simply be children, whatever course that might take. The adults were certainly negligent by most standards, but among this group, negligence was held in pretty high regard.

I read Robert Stone's memoir of his 1960s experiences and exploits. A contemporary of my mother, he too had young children, contemporary to my brothers and me. Children to whom he almost never directly referred or discussed in the raucous and drug-addled picture his book, *Prime Green*, painted. Until at last, on page 204 when he described a farewell party for his family and him before they moved to England. The party was also a farewell for a graduate student who had taken nitrous oxide while bathing and "slipped beneath the water to rise…never." According to Stone, there was nothing somber about this memorial. In the sixties, in certain parts of California, among a certain crowd of people, apparently things that might have been considered tragic were simply celebrated in kind. In this case, with a full supply of the leftover nitrous oxide that killed its original owner. Stone breaks into his narrative of the party with this: "All right, our kids were with us. Everybody's kids were with them. So we were doing gas with balloons, and you know how kids are with balloons. I mean you had to be there. It was a beautiful day. The kids were having such fun! There was so much gas. And it was hardly as though the late owner of the gas were lying there drowned in the bathtub; he had passed on, and he certainly didn't require any more gas."

It was a beautiful day. It was such fun. The dead don't care. As I read these lines, I heard my mother's voice saying the same things. Stone writes this passage as a "confession," acknowledging "few readers will fail to experience outrage at what I now feel bound to disclose" about feeding his own young children nitrous oxide. My confession, certainly not equal to his and yet paradoxical nonetheless, was that I found myself, unexpectedly, to be one of those few readers without outrage. Even though I never did drugs as a child, I was, as I imagine his children were, more than merely a survivor of many similar parties.

What I felt instead was pain that it took him to page 204 to turn his authorial gaze to his children. And then, only peripherally. For him, as for my mother, children were something to occasionally watch but not necessarily to watch over.

And here was the rub for me. On those nights coming back from some party, when I was curled like a woodland animal in the footwell of the passenger's side seat of my mother's Volkswagen, quivering in cold and nervousness, watching my mother's hands clench and unclench the steering wheel as she leaned forward toward the windshield, concentrating against the darkness of the night, the haze of the beer and wine she'd drunk, I frequently imagined what it might feel like if the car began to slide off the highway or careened off a cliff. Now I finally realized that the person I had been fearful for was not myself but my mother and my mother alone. My agony was not that I coveted some idea that she would suddenly begin to watch over me; I was simply overwhelmed with what I felt was the requirement that I watch over her.

Fashion

My mother was looking for her keys. She had already turned over the piles of paper on her desk, reached into the pockets of her jeans, and scrabbled with her long fingers into the corners of her purse. I had scoured the kitchen counters, looked into the glove box and floor of the car, and now I was standing outside her flurry of frantic and disordered energy, waiting to see what would happen.

She had her hands on her hips, her face pinched into a scowl that was not only about the keys but about being late for work, being irritated at her boss, being mad that some failure had left her with me, an inert six-year-old who for some reason I can't recall was not only not going to school today but was unable to help. I didn't know what to do to find her keys, fix her boss, make time move backward so she wouldn't have woken up late, she wouldn't have stayed up late, she wouldn't have ended up a single mother, approaching forty, who was juggling three kids and a job and a house without the help of a nanny, a man, an occasional child support payment, or the star status that all the accomplishments of her youth and the promise of the freewheeling sixties had seemed to guarantee.

She turned her purse upside down on the kitchen table. A gold-cased lipstick, a fat pink tube of mascara, a purple wallet, a few crumpled tissues, creased receipts, a tampon, a battered address book with a torn spine and a cover rubbed raw, an evil-looking plastic hairbrush with clusters of bent bristles, a pack of Pall Mall reds, a broken cigarette, and a cascade of tobacco fragments filtered down. Then, miraculously, out of a side pocket, the keys.

"C'mon, Lolly," she said. "You'll have to come to work with me today. I'll give you some paper, and you can draw. You'll have to be good; if you're not, I'll get in trouble."

It seemed to me that she already was in trouble; that *we* were already in trouble. However, I always had the hope—evidence notwithstanding—that being good might keep a wide variety of troubles at bay. We drove downtown. She was silent, but her bright eyes darted around, glancing off the dashboard, the steering wheel, the man at the corner, the car coming from the other direction, the one racing through the red light, me. At stop signs, she pulled the rearview mirror toward her and checked her makeup, wiped away a dollop of mascara, dabbed at a bit of goo in the corner of her eye, reapplied her lipstick, smacked her lips together, tugged at a stray strand of hair, wet her fingers against her tongue, and turned a curl against her cheek. She reached into her bag, extricated the brush, and started batting at my hair. I leaned away. The light turned green. She tossed the brush at me.

"OK, do it yourself. But brush your hair. You have to look nice."

I didn't care what I looked like. Especially as I began to realize that any time someone told her she had a beautiful daughter, she scowled until the person added, "But of course, look at her mother." Then her face would light up.

I dragged the stiff, plastic bristles against my head a few perfunctory times and placed the brush back in her bag.

Downtown was quiet. The empty streets seemed another reprimand; I wondered how many people were already inside the blocky industrial buildings. We entered one and went up a commercial elevator with a heavy black gate into a large room with a rough floor and windows set high in the walls just below the ceiling. One wall was lined with deep shelving that housed layers upon layers of cut fabric. There was a large table in the center of the room, tall enough for an adult to work at standing up, wide enough to accommodate a bolt of fabric, long enough to lay out a dozen pattern pieces. Resting on its side was a black appliance with a long cord stuck into a bulky fixture overhead and a blade long enough to cut through a tall stack of layered fabric.

The room seemed oddly quiet; the only noise came from an intermittent drone of needles punching fabric at one of the sewing machines stuffed into the corners of the room, where brown-skinned, black-haired, shapeless women hunched over the plate-sized circles of light that dropped onto their machines from dark, gooseneck lamps. There was one rolling rack of unfinished clothing stranded off to the side of the room. There was no glamour, no bustle, almost no color. I didn't see how this drab space could have anything to do with the energetic, color-saturated, high-fashion drawings that filled my mother's sketchbooks. I didn't see how this was connected to the full-page ads she showed us in newspapers with her name printed alongside an image of a heavily made-up woman in a showy frock camping for the photographer. It dawned on me that this is what my mother meant when she said, her voice laced with distaste, "downtown."

My mother gave me some paper and pens and pointed to a small table. She sat on a stool at a drafting table nearby. By glancing up, I could see the familiar arch of her back, the movement of her arms, and the tilt of her head that told me she was sketching. She reached occasionally into a tub of colored markers, and I heard them squeak against the paper as she added hues to her work. When she was working, her absorption created a space in which I could stop worrying. She became quiet, focused, her eyes flashing with intelligence and ideas. These were things I instinctively admired and longed for, not only for her but also in some small, dreamy way for myself. I already loved the steadying quality of having a task in front of me, something I found every day at school; I already hoped that her work could save her from the other, darker aspects of herself.

I sat near one of the sewing machines. The woman working there stole looks at me every time she adjusted a garment. In Spanish, under her breath, she whispered, "What a pretty little girl." In Spanish, I thanked her. My mother's helpers had taught me not only the language but also manners.

The elevator came up and the door slid open, noisy metal against metal. My mother straightened her back, and the other women tucked their heads closer to their sewing machines. A man with salt-and-pepper hair, pocked skin, and a large nose, wearing a tie with the sleeves of his white shirt rolled up above the elbows, strode into the room. I ducked my head, too. But my mother twisted the upper half of her body toward the man, a flower to the light. She lifted her chin, lowered her eyelids, and smiled at him. From beneath my half-closed eyelids, I saw him pause, an almost imperceptible hiccup in his forward motion, and then he kept coming toward her. He stood at her drafting table and flipped through her drawings. They talked about colors, seasons, hem lengths. He rubbed some small samples of cloth between the flat pads of his big fingers. They went over to the rack of clothes and pulled off a dress. He said something about the bias, the trim, the neckline. My mother nodded, pointed at something on her drawing, tapped her pen on the table, tugged at a sleeve on the unfinished dress, and forced it into place. I held my breath.

The man said, "OK," rather loudly—both a question and a statement—and then turned to leave. His eye caught on something out of place. Me. At the sudden cessation in his footsteps, my mother lifted her eyes from the dress she was considering.

"That's my daughter, Laurel," she said, her voice an uncharacteristically gentle sound around my real name, my full name, instead of the nickname my brother had given me as a toddler unable to get his tongue around the vowels in Laurel.

"I hope you don't mind. My baby-sitter is sick today."

I had no baby-sitter. She'd gotten in a fight with the woman who was most recently staying in the maid's room, a woman who didn't respond to her taunts and yelling but had simply seemed to shed something heavy as she walked out the door.

"She'll be no bother," my mother said to the man.

He looked at me, considering something.

"Lolly," my mother said, "say hello to Mr. Schwartz. Mr. Schwartz is my boss."

I mumbled a hello; he nodded.

Then, "Do you know," he said to me, his voice a deep hole, "how talented your mother is?"

I wasn't sure what talent was, but I knew my mother had it because it was what everyone said about her. I also wasn't sure what value talent offered. It seemed something innate, a thing given rather than earned. I suspected talent got you somewhere, but you needed something more to keep yourself there. Or move somewhere else.

With my mother and Mr. Schwartz staring at me, I knew what the right answer was, the answer a good girl would give. It also happened to be the truth.

"Yes," I said, nodding. Yes, I knew my mother was talented.

He bobbed his head in acceptance of my presence and left the room. Not too long after, my mother surprised me by packing up her things.

"C'mon, let's get out of here," she said.

Everyone else was still working. The sun was still high. I must have looked at her curiously.

"C'mon. He's gone for the day." Then, staring at me, shrugging, "I've done more than enough work. I'll finish up at home."

But once in the car, she started crying. "I hate that man," she hissed.

I waited a moment and then hazarded, "He seems to like you."

"He doesn't understand anything!" she wailed. "He's just another vulture trying to make a buck off my talent. I hate people like him. They have no talent of their own, so they're always trying to steal someone else's."

This was my mother's chronic complaint: I never get any credit, I never get any recognition, I'll show them, those grasping Jew bastards. She seemed to think, or had been convinced, that her talent had been bestowed on her because she was uniquely deserving of it. And that it should be more than enough. Everyone else wanted things like work and diligence and flexibility and compromise as well. All of which were things she spat upon. And all of which were things I valued before I was even old enough to understand what they were.

* * *

One day, some number of months or maybe even a year later, we were driving down Sunset Boulevard, my half brother in the front seat, my brother and me in the back, when my mother pulled over into a parking spot near the corner of Doheny. There was nothing here for us—only expensive clothing boutiques, nightclubs, an overpriced health food restaurant that my mother said had shitty service and tasteless food. My brothers and I waited, watching, while she got out of the car, put her hand on her hip, and, cocking her head back and forth as she did when she was drawing, considered something across the street. It was a new, bright white, stucco, one-story building with several large, dome-shaped windows. In each, a garment hung with arms and legs and hems outstretched and pinned in place with invisible filament. A sheer, floral dress with flared sleeves and layered skirts was in one window. There was a black lace minidress in another. Bell-bottom hip huggers paired with a patterned shirt in another. Our mother looked from the building to the cars cruising down Sunset. Some vehicles moved quickly, clearly on their way to somewhere else. Others crawled, their occupants leisurely looking out the windows or the open top of a convertible.

"What are we doing?" Jason asked.

I rarely questioned my mother about even the most mundane things, fearing her sharp word or sudden change in mood. My brothers were better humored and braver, especially Jason, who could almost always make her laugh. He was her darling, her favorite, she told everyone. After all, they were both Geminis, she said. They were twins. I was relieved to be a Libra, my birthday at the opposite, downward end of the summer.

She took her time answering. She continued looking from the street to the store. "I want to see if any cars slow down, if anyone stops to look."

"At what?"

I thought my brother was pushing it, almost challenging her, but her response came out strong, neutral, and with just the slightest hint of impatience.

"At the store," she said. Then after a moment, "Those are my clothes. See those two dresses? Those are my designs. This new store has started carrying my clothes. I'm only working for myself now. No more asshole bosses."

Our mother had started her own line. At home, she showed us a long, narrow box that held the clothing labels she had made. They were embroidered with her distinctive, looping, upright signature surrounded by a ribbon that tied a small bouquet of flowers at either end. She'd turned the dining room into a workroom, with an extra tall table where she rolled out long bolts of fabric, layer upon layer of cloth, on top of which she would arrange the seemingly abstract shapes of heavy manila paper that were patterns to parts of clothing. She had an industrial machine with a fat, cracked cord and a dangerous-looking blade that she used to cut into the stack of fabric, which she then handed to a seamstress who could decipher the code in the pattern shapes and turn them into pants, dresses, blouses. There was a cardboard barrel bigger than a garbage can in the corner, stuffed with bolts of fabric like some kind of absurd flower arrangement. A savage-looking, four-pronged hook hung in another corner, holding nothing more sinister than pattern pieces waiting to be pressed into service. Henry carved my mother a wooden sign, following the design of her dress label, which hung over our front door. He made her a pair of swirling silver gates—my mother called them "Deco"—which he installed on the open archway between the foyer and the dining room–turned-workroom.

We were told the gates were to keep us children out. We were driving her crazy. We were keeping her from her work. My brothers and I sometimes stood with our hands or chins resting on the swirled metal tubes, watching as she sketched, cut pieces of fabric, tugged, pinned, tucked a garment. She was continually looking for where she had last placed a pair of dark scissors with blades as long as my forearm. We were not allowed to touch these scissors, she told us, but especially never to use them on anything other than fabric. She demonstrated why, showing us how the heavy, black shears had been damaged by one of us who used them to cut the rough texture of paper, and now the shears shredded instead of sliced through a piece of filmy cloth. She told us how much it cost to have them sharpened—a seemingly staggering figure—and I looked upon them with new respect and the nascent concept of the intrinsic value of good tools.

She said that we couldn't touch the fabrics and patterns when they were laid out on the tall table. I asked if I could have scraps for my own sewing projects, and she said yes, but only from the floor or the garbage barrel. She told us we had to leave her alone and be very quiet when men came to the house with briefcases of books filled with slips of fabric that she rubbed between her fingers and then laid side by side in different combinations.

Now Mommy would be home all the time, she said. Now Mommy would be able to reach her full potential. Now Mommy would be the famous fashion designer her previous jobs and the newspaper pages printed with her designs under the department store banners had only hinted at.

It seemed exciting and serious. I was happy and hopeful for her. For us. Now Mom could get down to work.

I watched as my mother filled pad after pad of paper with drawings, and I held some part of my ambition and longing in check. When she wasn't in the room, I'd flip through the sketches of dresses and pants and skirts and ponchos, along with bags and boas and boots. I'd touch the small pieces of cloth that she'd pin to the corner of a page and imagine the flat images coming alive into three dimensions of fabric that moved and swung off the body. Mexican women translated her sketches into individual shapes of heavy manila paper, which, in turn, they laid down on a long swath of muslin. The pieces were then cut out and pinned to a headless, legless, armless, size 8 dress form that rolled on wheels all over the dining room. Parts were folded back where they were too big; pleats and darts were tacked into place; hems were measured from the floor upward, using a purple yardstick. Then patterns were resized and laid out onto real fabric—a woven jersey in navy, a double layer of black lace and georgette, a splashy print with a skirt that had to be cut on the bias to get the swing just right—and a sample was made.

I hazarded questions from time to time. More often, I just watched and learned.

She hung a dress in the dome-shaped window in our living room where she met with buyers from department stores. I peered around the corner and hoped the men didn't notice the stains on the carpet or sit on the weak part of the sofa. She showed us newspaper articles with headlines that announced "Anne Ford's New Line for Fall" and advertisements that featured women wearing clothing we'd seen come to life in what had been our dining room.

When my mother was occupied in another part of the house, or in the mornings before she woke up, I collected scraps of fabric from the floor or the garbage can. Sometimes, I just held onto them, put them in a drawer, and caressed their various textures while I imagined the beautiful things I might be able to fashion out of these remnants of her creative pursuits. I asked her to show me how to thread one of the dark, industrial machines that we had in the breakfast room. I took some pieces of felt and stitched them on three sides into a rectangle, and then folded down the top edge. I cut an uneven length and sewed it to each side of the open end. I cut some flower shapes from a scrap of contrasting felt and hand-sewed them to the front. I had a purse.

I found a large remnant of a silky white fabric covered with orange and black butterflies, folded it into a triangle, slipped a tie to the point, wrapped the tips around my back, and wore my new halter top with a pair of cut-off shorts.

I fretted over the unfinished nature of my work. The seams were rough and showed outside rather than inside, the edges unraveled, the thread didn't quite match. I watched the Mexican women more closely and saw how they put the right sides of the fabric together before sewing. I asked my mother how to make a tie that looked smooth, and, in a rare moment of indulgence, she took the time to show me how to use a safety pin to turn a strap.

Her friends watched, amused. Sometimes they asked if she wasn't nervous about letting a girl of only seven years old work on such high-powered machines. She shrugged; I hadn't hurt myself yet. In a rare moment of agreement, I was unafraid for myself, too.

They asked her if she taught me how to sew. She said no, because she didn't sew herself; her sewing skills, she proclaimed,
were not up to the quality of her designs. Besides, she said, I had
her genes. As if that were more than enough, as if I couldn't possibly ask for anything else from her.

And I didn't. I just watched her. Not only how she pinned a
dress or cut something on the bias but also how she changed her
expression and body angles when a man took notice of her or
she wanted him to take notice of her to help increase his interest
in her designs. I watched how many times she filled her glass in
the evenings, how many days in a row she slept in, how deeply
her forehead creased against a hangover when she did get up. I
watched her turn away the Mexican woman when she arrived
for work, how the department store buyers showed up less frequently, bolts of fabric stayed static in their barrel in the corner,
stacks of fabric went uncut on the tall table.

I crept into her room when she wasn't there, opened the
drawers in her bathroom, picked through the baskets filled with
fat pink tubes of mascara, gold tubes of lipstick, compacts, jars of
creams and lotions, thin brushes that left a fine line of black at the
edge of an eyelid, shadows in blue, lavender, silver, and various
shades of brown. I looked at the boxes of menstrual pads, bottles
of douche, and tubes of lubricants, flipped through pages of adult
magazines sometimes littering the floor next to the toilet.

I wandered into her dressing room, slid open the small drawers of her marble-topped dressing table with the ornate handles,
picked up pieces of costume jewelry, held them to the light, tried
to imagine what kinds of events my mother may have attended
that had called for such things. I slipped silk scarves through my
hands, across my neck, put on some of her lipstick, and then,

startled by how the brilliant red contrasted with my pale face, took it off again, wiping at my lips with a tissue dipped in cold cream.

I pushed my way into the dark depths of her closet, through the clutter of brilliant, saturated colors, silks, velvets, rayons, cottons, smells musty and sharp. I looked at the stains in her lace underwear, the shiny beads coming unstrung from the front of a gown, the hem falling from the edge of a dress, the unrolled edge of a hat, the feathers that floated into the air from a bubble-gum pink boa, the broken heels on her shoes. I crawled to the farthest, darkest corner of the closet and sat, my arms around my shins, my chin resting against my knees, and breathed in the smell of everything she had been, everything I had missed. And I wondered what kind of woman I was going to be.

*　*　*

My mother's talent was as much an excuse as an asset. Talent was supposed to make up for her lack of discipline. Talent was a reason to avoid any quotidian or mundane task, such as making a meal or cleaning the house.

"It's too boring," she'd say. "A waste of my time and energy. I have more important things to do."

For her, anything domestic needed to be simultaneously dressed up and down. If grapes were to be eaten, they must first be set on a platter—even though it was undoubtedly chipped—and, so as not to leave unsightly stems behind, taken in small clusters, snipped off using special scissors embossed with the image of a bird, its beak a pair of delicately curved blades. Oysters were best smoked but might as well be served in the can with toothpicks, because there was no reason to dirty forks or a plate. The wine had to be red but should come cheaply and by the gallon.

My brothers and I grazed along with her and her friends or made ourselves tuna fish on crackers, soup from a can, grilled cheese sandwiches, peanut butter on celery sticks, yogurt, hard-boiled eggs. And because this was Southern California, we consumed an enormous quantity and variety of fresh fruit. Sometimes, if we talked about being hungry at the end of the day, our mother stuffed some bills into Owen's hand and sent us to the counter at Thrifty Drug Store on the corner of Sunset and Fairfax. Or, she might tell us to go to Kentucky Fried Chicken, just a block away, next to the liquor store, and while you're there, get me a pack of cigarettes and a bottle of wine, tell him it's for me, he'll give it to you. The man at the liquor counter always did give us the booze, the cigarettes. Then we'd come home laden with a big bucket of fried chicken, smaller containers of coleslaw and baked beans, and a pile of soft, slightly sweet, pale yellow rolls, along with a brown paper bag heavy with a jug of red wine and a couple packs of cigarettes in the bottom.

Owen was the one who talked to the man at the liquor store while I hid behind him or waited outside. He carried the burdened bag home, he held onto the money and onto our hands when we crossed the street. He let me sit at the very end of the counter at Thrifty's where I could see into the kitchen and talk to the cook who knew what I liked, winked at me, and brought me a plate of spaghetti without my having to order.

It wasn't just the age difference of six and seven years that made Owen distinct from Jason and me. His origins were mysterious. He had three ersatz fathers: one unknown, who might have been a famous producer; one who gave him his last name,

87

different from ours, but was now dead; and one rarely seen or heard from, now living three thousand miles away, whom he referred to as "Brent" and we called "Dad." Owen had dark skin, eyes, and hair, while my brother and I were blond, blue-eyed, fair complected. Even when he was only twelve, thirteen, fourteen, Owen already looked on us—his kid sister and brother—with eyes that were growing distant. And he already bore the brunt of our mother's increasingly frequent rages, sometimes stoically, sometimes fighting back, screaming just as loudly, storming out of the house just as dramatically, going where, we didn't know, and she didn't seem to care.

Occasionally, we kids tried to orchestrate an event that seemed like the type of thing we sometimes saw families on television doing, like making dinner together. One evening, once we were home with our buckets and bags of food, Owen reached up into the cabinets for plates and glasses, while I folded napkins and set out silverware, and Jason maintained the stream of talk, storytelling, and teasing that kept our mother entertained. We filled a pitcher with milk—cartons were deemed ugly and therefore not allowed on the table—and we put the food on platters. We pulled up the bent wood chairs, one of which Mom had painted bubble-gum pink, another lilac-blossom purple; the other two were still dark brown wood. She leaned against a counter, smoking a cigarette, sipping wine. She wasn't hungry. She was rarely hungry.

I crawled into a chair and perched on my knees to reach the table. As I stretched my arm out for a bowl of food, my elbow nudged my glass. It tipped and fell, splashing milk over a plate of food. The milk seeped across the flecked linoleum kitchen table, approaching its silver edge. I froze, my arm over the table, my mouth open. My brothers moved into action, pushing their paper napkins at the spill, giggling and maneuvering the liquid. My mother squealed my name in exasperation and threw a rag from the sink onto the table. She swatted at the mess, squeezed the rag out in the sink, and crushed her cigarette into an ashtray. In that moment of the toppled glass, her mood switched from light to dark, and whatever promise the evening held was gone.

"You spill everything, Lolly," she snarled. "Now you've ruined the meal." She crossed her arms over her chest. "That's it," she said, lowering her voice and emphasizing each syllable. "You are not allowed to have liquids, ever again."

Then she plucked her purse from the kitchen counter and strode out the side door. We listened, staring at our plates, to the sounds of her retreat: the reluctant engine turning over and over before catching, the gears grinding as they slammed into place, the whine of reverse as the car buzzed down the driveway. We waited for a moment or two for something, listening to see if the car returned; and then when nothing happened, we began to move, stiff and unsure, not speaking, each of us caught in our private and collective worry. We finished cleaning up the milk. We moved the food around on our plates. Thoughts of where my mother might have gone competed with another question that consumed me.

"Is, is…," I sputtered. "Is milk a liquid?"

My brothers nodded, absently.

"Is water a liquid?"

More nods.

"Is chocolate milk a liquid?" I tried, hoping my favorite drink would be spared condemnation.

They nodded again, both grave and amused.

Finally, Owen said, "Lolly, it's all a liquid. Everything you could ever drink is a liquid."

Tears sprang to my eyes. He patted my arm.

"Don't worry," he said. "She didn't mean it."

His touch made my tears come more quickly. Everything I had started by spilling the milk began to wash over me.

"She'll be back. Don't worry. She'll come home soon."

We ate our dinner. We cleaned the kitchen. We turned on the outdoor lights and, after staring out the windows, looking and listening for her car, locked the doors. Then, after a brief discussion about the relative merits of protecting our own safety versus managing her anger if she didn't have her house keys with her and found herself locked out whenever she did come home, we left the side door unsecured. We collected on her big bed and turned on the television. It was very late, the house gone dark for hours, when we finally heard the side door open and shut. My brothers ran down the stairs into the shining kitchen. I followed behind more slowly. At the sight of us, she squatted down and opened her arms.

By the time I got close, her arms were already full. Her lipstick was long rubbed off, and her eyes blurred with alcohol. She wept a bit onto my brothers' shoulders, called them her precious darlings, then stood up unsteadily and wandered off to bed.

We became accustomed to her lapses and disappearances.

There was the time she forgot to pick me up from my half day of morning kindergarten, and I waited in the schoolyard, bright with the flat light of a Southern California afternoon, watching as one child after another left the playground. I waited until my teacher came back from her lunch break, a look of alarm on her face, and took me to the office where phone calls were made. I waited when we returned to the schoolyard until a large black car I'd never seen before appeared at the curb; an unfamiliar young man with blond hair cascading around his shoulders opened a back door and called, fumbling my name. The car was full of strange faces, smiles plastered on at odd angles, and then, from the far side of the backseat, my mother's arms reached for me, her eyes blurry with alcohol, her lips slick with saliva, her voice thick with lament.

There was the time she left me playing in the sand at Santa Monica beach and wandered off to a bar on the boardwalk. I was so intent on my hurt at being abandoned with only my plastic bucket and shovel and the damp sand for company that I didn't notice the fog rolling in until it was too thick to see more than a foot in front of me. I left my toys and stumbled through the long stretch of sticky sand and oatmeal mists until I saw in the distance what I took to be a person but what turned out to be simply a piece of gymnasium equipment. Then her voice, my name, came muted through the thickened air, and suddenly her pink bathing suit became a bright spot in the fog, and she dropped onto her knees at my feet, alcohol wafting up from each wracked, fearful sob.

My brothers and I learned to be relieved if she came back the same night she went out rather than staying gone until the following morning, or if she came back alone rather than with some man, unknown to us, on her arm. If she came back sober. If she picked us up when she said she would. If she remembered us at all.

*   *   *

Another umbral presence sometimes shared our Fairfax Avenue home.

On those rare evenings when the gathering was small, just my mother and a few friends or neighbors, when the night had become dark but the drinking had been moderate, when the mood was more reflective than raucous and everyone was gathered in the living room, sitting cross-legged on the floor, leaning against the substantial pillows, or draped across the pale blue sofa, then stories about this creature might begin.

The scene was always the same. The dark blue, purple, and green Oriental rug would be cluttered with wine glasses and ashtrays, a stray shoe, a sleeping dog, a plate with crumbs, a curl of cheese drying on the edges, a can of sardines or clams with a couple of toothpicks floating in the oil. Candles stuck in a pile of wax on a broken plate or dripping down the sides of old wine bottles would give the room a fitful glow accentuated by the complete darkness in the rest of the house and punctuated by the red pulse of someone dragging on a cigarette, the sudden flare of someone else lighting a fresh one.

I would be just beyond the circle of adults, out of the dim aura of light, curled around a pillow, clutching my blanket, my face toward the candles, my back to the gloomy house. I drifted in and out of sleep, knowing I had to get up in some number of hours and get myself to Miss Siegel's first-grade classroom. I listened vaguely to the scattered bits of conversation and bubbles of laughter, my ear tuned, waiting for the tone of the voices to turn hushed and conspiratorial. Then I would shrug off sleep and turn my full attention to the adults.

One person said that when he walked by our house late at night, he saw a face at a window glimmering in the nimbus of its own light, even as the rest of the house was pitched in empty darkness. Another person, passing through the hallway, saw a dark-haired woman in a long white dress dash out of the bathroom and around the corner. When he followed her, he found no one. Someone else saw a similar figure running up the walk to our house in the half light of a late summer evening, and when he called to her, she evaporated.

In our house, doors sometimes flew open of their own accord. Windows lashed shut would be found flapping in the morning. Cool spots appeared and disappeared. Candle flames flickered in a nonexistent breeze. One night a mirror crashed to the floor, and when Henry went to investigate, he found its hook still in the wall. The television knob sometimes spun wildly through all the channels repeatedly, of its own accord. Our ghost was invariably described as having black hair, wearing a long white dress, and she was always, at first, mistaken for my mother.

She had never seen the ghost herself but still had her own stories to tell.

"You know how Mexicans are," she'd begin. "They have no fear of the dead. They celebrate death, spirits, the afterlife," she'd say, pausing while someone leaned across the rug with a candle to light the cigarette she shook up and out of the pack. "I had a pattern maker working for me once, and when I came home from an errand, she told me that she'd seen our ghost. She said she'd been in the house alone and heard footsteps running up and down the stairway."

Here, my mother would pause and take a deep drag of her cigarette, letting the smoke drift out her nose as she began again.

"She said she went into the foyer and asked the spirit why it was here, why it couldn't rest."

Another pause while my mother sipped her drink, drew out the suspense, made everyone wait.

"The ghost told this Mexican woman that she had neglected her own children when she was alive and, as atonement, was here to watch over my kids."

There would be a small moment of quiet where everyone seemed to consider not just this claim but how my mother would respond to the charge. She'd break the tension of the moment with a laugh.

"It's true," she'd say. "No one ever sees the ghost when the children aren't around. Have you noticed that? She only appears when they're here."

Then she'd go on with another story to prove the point. On a certain night at the end of a summer my brother and I had spent with our father in New Jersey, my mother was at home alone with a friend. She said they were in her workroom when they heard a window banging against the wall in another part of the house. They followed the sound, latched the window, and went back to their discussion. Then banging started in another part of the house. They went and secured that window, only to hear a door fling open and closed. They went to the sunroom, locked that door, and moved themselves to the living room. Then the man noticed a guitar near the fireplace and asked my mother who played.

"Before I could answer him," she'd say, "we both heard a single, loud strum. Then footsteps running away, through the house." She'd pause to stub out her cigarette. "The kids had been gone all summer, and no one saw the ghost while they were away. They were coming home the next day. The ghost came back just in time."

I thought of the ghost when I was extra careful using the big, blue-tipped matches to light the stove. I thought of her when I wandered the house late at night, snuffing out cigarettes still smoldering in ashtrays, blowing out candles left burning, and locking doors left open. I tried to conjure her presence when I woke in the middle of the night to the sound of my mother's body, softened by alcohol, falling from the handrail to the wall and back again as she fought her way up the stairs, while

I lay in bed hoping the ghost could somehow keep her moving down the hall to her own room instead of stopping in mine. Which she invariably did, slumping down in a heap, dropping her clumsy hand against my face again and again, telling me, her breath heavy with alcohol and smoke, how I was her baby doll, her Darling Lolly Dolly, even though I didn't appreciate her, didn't understand all she'd done for me, all she'd been through, even though I wouldn't play with dolls, didn't like dresses, wasn't entertaining like my brother. And then when I begged her to go to bed, told her I needed to sleep, I had to go to school in the morning, she would push herself up, grip the doorjamb, and spit the words *bitch* and *witch* at me before resuming her stumbling way down the hall.

One night when the house was in a strangely deep quiet, I woke from the depths of a dream of falling through the sky to discover that I really was falling, slowly, gently tumbling out of bed, tangled in my sheets, which clung to the mattress and slowed my descent, cushioning my crash to the floor. I landed, swaddled, just inside my bedroom doorway. I was facing out into the hallway, and as my eyes opened from the fog of sleep onto the stillness of the house, I saw my mother running toward me, her long white nightgown a diffuse glow in the darkness. She kneeled at my side, loosened the covers, and lifted me back to the mattress. She rearranged the bedding and tucked me into a snug cocoon. She sat on the edge of the bed, and I rolled slightly toward her weight, her warmth. She brushed the thin strands of fine hair from my forehead with a gentle fingertip. As I was falling back asleep, I felt her leave me.

The next morning I tiptoed downstairs and wandered the house, stepping over one or more of my mother's friends sleeping on the sofa or among the cushions on the floor, and began my regular weekend morning ritual. I blew out candlewicks still burning in a pool of wax melted over the piano top or on a marble side table, collected glasses stained with small rings of dried red wine, emptied ashtrays brimming with lipstick-lined cigarette butts into brown bags from Ralph's grocery store. I filled the sink with hot water and, standing on a stool, dipped the glasses into the suds and watched the soap bubbles turn pink with leftover wine. I washed, rinsed, and then lined up the glasses and the dishes in the drain tray, slowly, carefully, so they would not chip or break as so many had done already under less steady hands. I put large spoonfuls of coffee grounds into a white enamel pot, filled it with water, set it on the stove, lit the burner, and turned the flame down low so the coffee would simmer without boiling over and making another mess. I poured the thick, brown liquid through a dented strainer into the large, shallow mug that was my mother's favorite and then lifted the heavy milk bottle and poured it into the mug until the coffee was pale and cool. As I did what I had done so many times before, I thought of my nighttime visitation and allowed myself the smallest of hopes that this might be the start of something new.

I pulled and pushed myself up onto the counter to get her white, wicker breakfast tray with the pockets on either side from a high shelf. I cracked ice, put several shattered cubes into a glass, and filled it with water. I got a fringed lavender napkin from the drawer and placed it on the tray along with the glass of water, the cup of coffee, and a piece of toast. With my arms stretched in front of me, I took careful steps through the still-quiet house, up the stairs, down the long hall to her bedroom, thinking, wondering what I might say to her. I turned my back to her door and slowly pushed it open. I looked carefully at the rough shapes under the white linens stained red, black, and blue with makeup, trying to ascertain if there was one body or two in the bed. I tiptoed into the room and set the tray on the floor near her bed, trying not to look at the black hair flung across her cheek, stuck to the corner of her mouth, flayed over the pillow.

Most days, I didn't want to wake her. I didn't want to face her cranky with a headache, or worse, in a benevolent mood, smiling, reaching for me, pulling me into her stale odor and sticky lips. I didn't want to expose her, once again, to my own resistance to her. Most days, I'd make a silent retreat, threading my way through the ashtrays, feather boas, velvet pants, purple suede heels, and vibrant, silky underthings that littered the floor. But this day, I perched on the edge of her bed, just beyond the reach of her arms, and waited for her to emerge from the sheets and pillows to open her eyes. The smell of the coffee roused her. She threw her arm out from under the covers and lifted her creased face from the pillow marked with yesterday's makeup. She pushed herself up in bed, blinked against the morning light, and tugged at her twisted nightgown. She ran the back of her hand over her mouth and wiped the rime that she found there on the sheets. She looked at me as if she could not quite recall who I was. She reached for the mug, cradled the cup in both her hands, closed her eyes, and took a large swallow of the milk-cooled coffee.

"What?" she said after a moment.

I wasn't quite ready to respond.

"What do you want, Lolly? Why are you looking at me like that?"

I twisted at my waist. I looked at my hands, my fingers with the bitten nails laced in my lap. What did I want? I wanted the night before to have been real.

"I, I just wanted…," I started, stumbling. Whatever words I had planned to say fled when faced with her irritation. I finally managed to whisper, "I just wanted to thank you for coming to get me last night."

She kept looking at me, her forehead muddled with remnants of sleep and confusion.

"When I fell out of bed," I added, hoping to clear her brow.

She pushed her eyebrows together between thumb and forefinger. She took another slug of coffee and put the mug back on the tray. She drank the glass of water down.

"I have no idea what you're talking about," she said finally, sliding back under the covers. "I didn't come and get you last night. I didn't even know you fell out of bed."

She rolled away from me, pulling the blanket up over her shoulder, burying her face.

I remained in the empty space her words left behind.

"It must have been a dream," I said.

I walked away, closing the door quietly behind me.

I was young enough to believe that what had happened the night before had been real. It just wasn't her. I was also old enough to know that when I left her room, I left some part of my hope for her behind. In its place, the possibility of hope for me began to stir.

$\mathcal{J}ames$

During our years living at the house on Fairfax, my mother's parents, Daisy and James, lived about an hour's drive from us in a small, single-story ranch house perched over a hillside on stilts, at the end of a cul-de-sac, framed in front by a low, white fence. The far wall of the living room held multiple glass windows and doors that opened out onto a concrete patio and a view my grandmother swooned over. She'd clasp her hands in pleasure at the endless horizon of miniature houses spread across the plain below, twinkling at night like a blanket of stars.

However, no matter how much my grandparents clucked encouragement at me, I was scared to go near that side of the house, frightened that my small weight would create a catastrophe and send the house and all of us tipping and then rushing down the hillside.

For inadequately explained reasons—something about her being heavier than he, which caused the mattress to tip—my grandparents had separate bedrooms. His was at the front of the house with a mattress set directly onto the floor; hers was in the back, a smaller, darker room with a tall bed and an overstuffed closet that she'd open for me from time to time, dragging out wooden boxes that contained the silver her family bought her as a wedding present but she never used. She showed me pearls that had belonged to her sister, a necklace of gold beads to which she'd add a new bead every year, and a diamond ring she'd had made from a stone my grandfather had bought for another woman, only to break off that engagement to marry my grandmother instead. She'd lift items out one by one and intimate that all this might one day be mine. When I was older, more mature. When I'd proven myself, I thought, to be unlike my own mother, who had lost every piece of valuable jewelry she'd ever been given.

Jason and I spent many weekends at this house, and in the summer spent weeks at a time. Owen already had his own teenager-trying-to-be-an-adult life. He was rarely home anymore. He came and went, but mostly went.

My grandmother would pick us up in her dark blue Thunderbird, pulling halfway up the driveway that was almost too narrow for the expanse of her car, and beep the horn. We all wanted to avoid the inevitable confrontation that so often ensued during even the most fleeting contacts between our mother and grandmother; they were locked in an epic and completely stalled symbiosis of dread and need and resentment of each other. But we were frequently late, not packed up, my hair not brushed, and so Grandma would walk up to the side of the house, open the door, and "Hallo" inside without stepping farther than the laundry room or kitchen. We'd yell through the house to her, rush around to gather our few things, and then appear in the kitchen, our mother lagging behind, holding her robe closed with her balled-up fist.

A few words would pass between the women. Theirs was a covert code of veiled suggestions, hints, questions, and requests that usually had something to do with money—which our grandmother had and our mother didn't. Because our grandmother was a "penny pincher" and our mother was a "spendthrift." Because our grandmother grew up poor on a hardscrabble farm back East in Vermont and managed her way through the Depression, and our mother had been given every advantage possible and was spoiled rotten. Because our grandmother was hardworking and our mother self-indulgent.

Standing there just inside the side door, if she wasn't careful and didn't catch herself, Grandma might shoot a few tentative glances into the house, toward the dishes in the sink or, even worse, still on the table; an unfamiliar person wandering past a doorway, cigarette stuck to lower lip; the empty cutting table in the dining/work room; to my mother's unwashed, undressed self, even though it was the middle of the day.

"What are you looking at?" Mom would snap.

Grandma would sniff and blink in the glare of this outburst, her head quaking almost imperceptibly like a lone leaf on an empty tree.

Without waiting for an answer, or because she already knew the answer, my mother would lash out: "Stop prying! Stop being so judgmental, so damn controlling. Just get the kids out of here and leave me alone."

Grandma would shoo us out the door, and we'd all scuttle down to the car, bent forward as if anticipating hurled objects.

Once we were around the corner and out of sight, Grandma would start talking in a nervous ramble about the lamb chops she'd found at Safeway for three cents less a pound than what they'd had at Ralph's, what she thought she'd broil for dinner because that was, after all, the healthiest way, wouldn't we like a nice baked potato with our chops because if we didn't use sour cream it wasn't really that bad for us, but of course, the sour cream was the best part, and why didn't she pick up some ice cream for dessert because she had to go to the drive-through dairy for another gallon of milk just to have it on hand. Then she'd start singing us songs she remembered from her own childhood, and slowly, her hands would twist less frequently on the steering wheel and the tight line of her mouth would loosen as she gave full voice to a ditty about the "washy, washy, all the day washy" Chinese laundryman.

The minute we got to her house, Grandma started making plans to go back out. There were always errands to run, trips to the pool or park, shopping to do, a list of things that needed to be checked off a green-paged spiral notebook she kept next to the phone.

"Who wants to come to the store with me?" she'd say.

Jason always said yes. I always shook my head no. I didn't want to go shopping, trying on clothes, riding around in the car, playing on the contraptions at the park. She'd ask me if I was sure, didn't I want to go out to a nice lunch somewhere, didn't I want to see if there were some clothes on sale, something on special? Could she bring me something back from the store? Did I need anything? I simply shook my head again and asked only for some toast before she left. White bread, the inside doughy, the crisp outside softened by what she called oleomargarine. Two slices, each cut twice in both directions into nine small squares, set on a turquoise or pale-peach Fiestaware plate. Then, after she and Jason left, I would walk down the hall that ran through the center of the house holding the plate out in front of me. Past my grandfather's bedroom; the bathroom with the red, flocked wallpaper where my grandmother sat me in the tub to wash my hair and douse it with globs of pink, Breck cream rinse; past the bedroom with the twin beds where my brother and I slept, the bedroom where my grandmother slept; to the end, where the last door opened onto a laundry room with a washer and dryer, a small window, a closet, and a door that led into a tiny backyard, enclosed by a high fence.

Here, tucked against a small patch of wall between the door and the closet, there was a compact desk of caramel-colored wood. This is where I would find my grandfather, his knees bracketed by the three drawers down each side; gooseneck lamp, mechanical pencils, gum eraser, compass, three-sided ruler, and other devices I didn't know the use of spread around the terse desktop. I tiptoed into the room, barely looking at him. Without lifting his head, he acknowledged my presence by nodding ever so slightly toward a small chair next to the desk. Gingerly, I settled there, my feet dangling above the floor, the plate in my lap, and, chewing slowly, methodically ate one small piece of toast at a time, licking the crumbs off my fingers in between.

From time to time, I would flick my eyes sideways to his desk, watching as he extended the fat lead in his silver mechanical pencil, lifted and examined the different sides of his triangular ruler before settling it down on the page, used a metal form to outline perfect geometric shapes on graph paper so pale green it looked like it had been left out in the sun. I stretched out the eighteen squares of toast as long as I could and ran the last buttery morsel around the plate to pick up all the crumbs. It was as if I considered the time it took to eat the toast the only time allotted me to be with him. I didn't know what he was doing, what his tools were for, how to translate what he was putting on the paper into something concrete. It didn't matter; I was content to sit in the quiet space created by someone focused on the purposefulness of work.

Eventually Grandma would come back, my brother in tow, telling stories of what she had spent and what she had saved, loaded up with bags of boys' clothing and food for an already overflowing freezer. Her arrival broke the silence I had experienced with my grandfather. I was disappointed and also relieved, craving but also unused to the concentrated quiet I experienced with him. Like a very hungry person being given food, I could take it only in small quantities.

My grandmother asked my grandfather how I'd been, did he mind having me around?

"She's no bother," he'd say, dismissive, preoccupied.

It was a response that satisfied me. I took more pride in being a presence that could be ignored than I would have of his attentions.

* * *

One year my mother insisted on having Thanksgiving at our home on Fairfax Avenue. She invited her parents and her older, darker, more brooding brother. We spent the day attempting to clean, or at least reorder, the house. We flung open the windows, turned up the stereo, threw our clothes into closets. We rubbed at the multicolored crayon marks Jason and I had drawn on the walls and floor of our room to divide our shared territory. We scraped wax from candles that had melted over tables, wiped the kitchen counters, threw away full ashtrays and empty bottles. We put bolts of fabric back into the barrel, piled patterns up under the dressmaking-turned-dining table, which we then covered with an ad hoc tablecloth made from a sweep of purple fabric. We collected mismatched silverware from drawers cluttered with wine corks and pieces of broken china that someone was supposed to glue together someday and set the table with dishes of different patterns and sizes. We had only a couple of stools that were tall enough to allow an adult to sit properly at the high worktable, so we pulled up regular chairs and piled phone books onto the seats. I said I could kneel on a chair. Owen and Henry offered to stand.

My mother's eyes flashed with an unfamiliar anxiety. The child my mother might have once been revealed herself in a few fleeting glimpses of a person trying to prove something, hoping for approval, knowing before she even began that she was doomed not to get it. This vestigial insecurity was always covered with so many layers of bravado; now I was seeing the shadow of a wary animal picking its way through treacherous woods.

Grandma and Grandpa arrived. My uncle was late. He too was dubbed a genius, and a bastard, a piano prodigy unable, or perhaps unwilling, to work for reasons never fully explained but grudgingly indulged. He drove a cab. He gave astrology readings to little old ladies who answered his small ad. He lived in the house his parents bought for him. He had a large head and a mane of thick, sooty hair that hung over heavy eyebrows set over inky eyes that never smiled. When he and I were in the same room, someone would invariably remark, "Isn't it so funny that these two have the same birthday and yet hate one another?" I didn't think he hated me in particular; he simply seemed to dislike everything, especially children. And I didn't dislike him; I found him impenetrable. Whereas my mother turned everything outward into a show, a party, a pose, he turned it inward into a black hole of unvoiced resentment. I was afraid of being sucked into his dark vortex.

He finally arrived, we took our places at the table, and my grandparents sipped primly at glasses of wine while my mother wrung her hands in the kitchen. One of the dishes didn't come out as expected. Not everything was done at the same time. There were sizable lumps in the gravy. There was some confusion about what my grandmother had brought or was supposed to bring. Snarling to Henry, my mother listed her complaints against her mother: she brought too much, she duplicated something my mother was trying to make, she interfered on purpose, she couldn't leave her alone, she didn't trust her to make her own Thanksgiving meal. My mother's dish did fail, but my grandmother's dish was judged too bland, a poor replacement, just like everything she did, she's always trying to copy me, but she can't, went the muttered lament.

My brothers and I tiptoed into and then back out of the kitchen, trying to help. My mother was fighting a losing battle against her own tears. Henry put his arm over her shoulders and kept her glass filled.

Eventually, we were enlisted to bring trays of food to the table. My grandfather carved the golden brown turkey, complaining once or twice under his breath about the not-sharp-enough knife. He asked whether I wanted light or dark, and when I hesitated because I didn't know the difference, he dropped a hunk of meat onto my plate. My mother asked for the "pope's nose," and my grandmother winced, saying the tail was a fatty, disgusting part of the bird, accusing my mother of choosing it as a provocation.

Henry went to top off my grandparents' wine but was rebuffed. My uncle and grandfather sent significant looks toward my mother's glass, which had been filled and emptied several times already. My grandfather made a remark, audible only to my grandmother, who patted his arm, clenched her teeth into a stiff smile, and whispered, "Please, don't start." Clipped comments and low verbal jabs were slung across the table between my grandfather, uncle, and mother. Money, favoritism, lazy, spoiled, good-for-nothing, drunk....

My grandmother worked her husband and son, trying to calm them. My brothers and I kept our heads down. Then, my uncle threw his napkin into his plate, shoved back from the table, and told his father to go to hell. My grandmother asked him to sit back down and, please, don't ruin the meal. My grandfather told him to leave, go ahead, get out. My mother said her father was a bully, a prick. He said she was ungrateful, a spoiled brat, a ruined woman. The adults suddenly stood and moved away from the table. Grandma threw kisses at my brothers and me as she hustled behind Grandpa.

Doors slammed a momentary quiet into the house. Gravy soaked darkness into the purple cloth of my uncle's napkin. The silence was broken with my mother's sobs. Her tears dripped off her cheeks onto the dry turkey and glistening yams. Henry comforted her with a bottle of wine, a pack of cigarettes, and a retreat to a dark corner of the house. My brothers and I cleaned up the debris.

* * *

My grandfather died when I was six years old. It was sudden, unexpected, a heart attack. (A similar fate befell his son, my uncle, no more than a year or so later—he was playing piano, and his girlfriend heard a thud when he fell to the floor.) My grandmother said my grandfather had always been worried about his health because his own father had a bad heart, which was why he lifted weights, took so many vitamins, and was careful about his diet. At the funeral, before the service started, Jason and I looked at our grandfather lying in his coffin and swore to each other that we saw his eyes move. During the service, my mother shed a few tears and gripped my hand ferociously. Thieves broke into my grandparents' house while we were at church. After discovering the broken window in the laundry room, Grandma rushed to her closet. The silver and jewelry had remained undiscovered. I felt a wave of selfish relief.

A year or so after my grandfather's funeral, my mother and grandmother took Jason and me to the bank. They showed us a binder with a variety of small booklets and told us to pick one, each. Jason got something geometric; I chose purple swirls. We waited in chairs until a man came out from a desk behind a little gate with our registers. Our grandmother showed us our names and a number printed in blue ink on the inside. She explained that our grandfather had left our mother and us some money when he died. Our mother, my grandmother said without looking at her, was going to watch over our inheritance for us. If we ever wanted a toy or a book or something like that, we could purchase it with our own money, my mother added. All we had to do was ask. As proof, they took us to Quigley's, a five-and-dime across the street, where we each spent a few dollars on some small playthings.

I don't remember how many digits were in that number in that passbook. For most of my life, I didn't remember that it even existed. But a decade later, scrambling for college tuition, my father asked me what had happened to the money my grandfather had left me. Only then did I remember that once, when I was only eight years old, I'd asked my mother for some money, and when she returned my passbook to me along with a twenty-dollar bill, I noticed several numbers of three and four digits in the withdrawal column. I shook inside with fear that I had done something wrong, that my grandfather's money, which I'd been told over and over was accumulated by hard work and scrimping and saving and in spite of denying the girl my mother had once been absolutely nothing and never getting the acknowledgment he deserved, had been lost or disappeared or taken away.

At the same time, I knew I hadn't done anything wrong. I was just old enough to have a sense of justice swelling inside me. I was just old enough that some part of me wanted to catch my mother in a lie. But I was still young enough to cringe in anticipation of even the smallest outbursts of her fury. I swallowed against my dread and asked my mother what the numbers meant. She told me they didn't mean anything. Then she added, with exaggerated casualness, that she'd taken money out of my account.

"Lolly, it's OK."

My expression must have shown an unwillingness to accept her explanation.

"Lolly, the law says that if a child has money and the parent doesn't, it's OK for the parent to use the child's money. It's fine. I'll pay it back."

Her hands fluttered in the air like something set loose.

I never saw the passbook again.

I never saw my mother work again, either.

* * *

On a sunny weekend afternoon in the early seventies, my mother showed my brothers, me, and a few other kids who

109

were around the house a long piece of white-primed plywood. Someone had painted "Annie's Garage" in black, looping script, and she told us to decorate around the edges. We dipped brushes into small pots of paint and embellished the sign with multicolored daisies, spiky yellow suns with rainbows jutting off the sides, stars in many shapes and sizes, palm trees sprouting green fronds. She then directed us into every corner of the house, pointing out broken furniture, clothing we didn't wear anymore, books we didn't read, bolts of fabric with only remnants left, costume jewelry, feather boas and gowns left over from her modeling days, pottery she'd recently picked up on a trip to Tijuana, beaded headbands she'd bought at a flea market, and had us schlep everything out to the garage.

She hung rugs, tapestries, and cheap Indian bedspreads against the bare wood walls. She arrived one day with a tall, oak wardrobe sticking up out of the back of the open-topped Volkswagen Beetle. She filled its dozen or so drawers with sewing notions, rolls of lace and ribbons, cheap jewelry, broken plates that only needed gluing to be set right again, headbands, necklaces, and bracelets made by friends or picked up at other garage sales. Beaded flapper dresses, faded men's shirts, our worn-out castoffs, and old baby clothes hung from the beams overhead. She draped pieces of velvet over torn upholstery and arranged a chaise lounge so it offered a view down the driveway and other chairs so they offered views of the watercolors she displayed. The garage became a cluttered, mysterious, tattered yet sensuous, strange brew of a salon. She put up a sign that offered custom clothes and hand-painted portraits. Another sign, set up as a table tent, offered tarot card readings and massage. In a small room off the side of the garage, she put a metal cashbox inside a metal desk, found a lock for the latch on the door, and called it her office. She put up the sign we'd painted on the corner of the house: Annie's Garage, a permanent, always-open, completely groovy offering of junk and miscellaneous services.

People wandered in from the street, seemingly out of curiosity more than a desire to shop, but often enough they peeled a few dollars from their pocket for a tie-dyed piece of fabric to use in a costume, a showy ring that caught their eye, a beaded headband for a gift.

One afternoon, the bells my mother had hung on the gate she'd installed halfway down the driveway rang. She was on the phone and yelled at me to go see who was there. The man there was tall enough to rest his arms on top of the gates. He looked down at my uplifted chin and said he'd heard there was a woman here who could make custom shirts. I nodded and took him to the garage. My mother took out a tape measure and stretched it across various parts of his body, pulled some bolts of fabric from the barrel that had once been in the corner of our dining room and sketched a few designs on a pad of paper. He pointed, nodded, handed her some bills. When he was gone, she told me that I'd just met a famous basketball star, Wilt Chamberlain.

One regular visitor was a short man with a protruding belly, squinting eyes, and a string of long gray hair held back in a strip of leather. His arrival was always announced by the deep rumble of his black motorcycle with the extra tall handlebars and the extended front fork. He wore a black leather vest over his white T-shirt, blue jeans, and thick, black leather boots. For me, he always had a sweet word and a welcoming lap. My mother did a painting of him, which he paid for but left hanging on the wall of the garage.

"Who's that?" someone invariably asked, pointing at the portrait.

"That's the head of the Los Angeles Hells Angels. He's a cus-tomer," she'd reply, in a tone mixing nonchalance with warning.

Henry brought home a carload of keg-size hunks of wood, which he lightly sculpted into abstract, vaguely organic shapes and then set up around the garage and driveway. He stuck price tags on them, but they were only used as a place to set an ashtray or grab a seat. Friends dropped off things they'd made: tie-dyed shirts, embroidered pants, leather and bead work. I had listened and watched other people do it enough times that when someone asked for a tarot card reading, my mother turned them over to me, which seemed to amuse as much as inform them. She took the bills they offered up when the reading was complete and stuffed them into her bra. Few things ever left Annie's Garage, but we needed little ourselves; my mother had her inheritance—as well as ours—and as often as not, her friends brought booze and cigarettes, and sometimes food.

I didn't know what my grandfather's death had deposited in her bankbook. Or ours. Or Owen's. But around this time, Owen began to change, racing ahead of his teenage years. His fights with our mother escalated. She hurled insults at him as if he were the adult that he pretended to be, and he volleyed from screaming back at her to dissolving into tears as he fled the house. He was rarely in school and only intermittently home. By the time he was fifteen, he dropped out of school completely and moved out of the house, was kicked out, or some combination of the two. We saw him from time to time when he was between friends or couches to sleep on. He had a sweetness to him that popped up on rare occasions with a sudden smile that showed the gap in his teeth, or when he ruffled my hair, asked me how school was going, and told me I was smart. He showed up to grab some food, join a party, pick up some clothes, spend a few nights, ask for money, and scream for it when asking didn't work. Screaming never worked either. Then he was gone again.

It was around this time, too, that Henry announced that he was going to France. He was going to retrieve some money from a business he'd once had there. He'd be back in a few months, and he'd take us all out to Barney's to celebrate. But he didn't come back. He bought a Laundromat in France instead. And got a new girlfriend.

My mother was left with a broken heart, a bad drinking habit, and two kids. Jason and I were left with each other. And to try to care for her.

* * *

In my memory, my grandfather was a man who rarely smiled, said little, combed his hair straight back from his forehead, wore brown leather slippers with a red lining, and washed down a dozen multicolored vitamins every morning with the fresh orange juice my grandmother squeezed for him.

When my mother spoke of her father, it was as an underappreciated genius and a controlling bastard. She offered two object lessons to back up her claims. He was a superior airplane engineer who had designed the first all-metal aircraft back in 1936 but had never gotten the credit he deserved from his boss or the industry; and, he had given her a black eye when, as a teenager, she had balked at participating in yet another beauty contest he'd signed her up for. To the second story, she always added a footnote about her own triumph. She not only went to the contest with her black eye, but she won. Because it was a Miss Legs contest, all the girls wore masks.

To me, this story was shocking not just because of the violence of my grandfather but because it was the first indication I had that perhaps my mother hadn't always sought out the spotlight, hadn't always been a willing participant in the creation of the persona she seemed to so fully embrace. It was the first suggestion that her parents were complicit in the person she became.

There was another story told about my grandfather. When he was a young teenager, he lived in Jamaica with his parents and several siblings—of English descent, my great grandfather had moved his family to the island for health reasons. My grandfather worked with his father, a dentist and inventor. One afternoon, father and son walked into their home and found it emptied of furniture other than a bed, a table, and a chair. There was a brief note. My great grandmother had sold all the furniture and taken herself and the other five children on a steamer to New York City.

When my grandmother told this story, she positioned her mother-in-law as a brave woman, a hero, really, who rescued her children from an irresponsible, itinerant adventurer of a father and took them to the promise of better education and opportunities offered in the United States.

"Can you imagine?" my grandmother would say. "The courage? At the turn of the century, with no money and five children, to do such a thing?"

She left her eldest son, my grandfather, it was said, because she didn't want to separate him from his father. They were so close. They were such good friends. They were working together. Whatever heartbreak James or his father may have experienced at this abandonment was never mentioned.

When I was twenty years old and in my last year at New York University, my grandmother mentioned that I had a cousin, really my mother's cousin, who lived in New York City. Perhaps I would be interested in meeting her. I was, and I did. Linda, who was only fifteen years older than I and lived a few blocks from NYU where I was attending college, invited me to dinner. After sharing our astonishment that neither her parents nor my grandmother had thought to tell us of the other's existence sooner, we became friends. And began sharing stories. Linda had a deep interest in her—now our—family history, especially the various inconsistencies, surprising mismatches, and fascinating globetrotting of her grandparents, my great grandparents, Henry and Rachel. James, my grandfather, was Henry's oldest son; Linda's father, Tom, was Henry's youngest.

Linda had learned that Henry was the product of a Jewish mother and an English father and that he and his many brothers left England in the early and mid-1800s to find their fortune in Central and South America, the United States, Canada, and elsewhere. Henry had married as a young man, but this first wife died in childbirth. Henry allegedly made substantial amounts of money at various times in his life working on inventions for corporations and then spent it pursuing his own projects. He and his family lived in South America, the Caribbean, and the United States. They moved to Jamaica when James was fourteen because Henry required a warmer climate for some health concern. Linda had heard that Henry quoted entire passages of Shakespeare at the dinner table but didn't have enough money to buy his children clothes or to send them to school. And that Rachel, his second wife, was illiterate.

I had a box of yellowed documents that fleshed out the story somewhat. And raised new questions. I had a vague memory of my mother going through this same shallow box filled with her father's papers many years earlier; Daisy had unearthed it from somewhere, and my mother was completely rapt, poring over every piece of paper. I can't recall how the box came to me. But over many years, I returned to this box again and again, fingering the various documents, occasionally letting them lead me on some research expedition or another. There were transcripts and official records about births, deaths, marriages; membership cards from the Society of Automotive Engineers, the American Helicopter Society, the National Aeronautic Association of USA, Redondo Evening High School; stamps cut off from envelopes; veterans exemption receipts; a bankbook from the late 1940s to early 1950 with deposits ranging from $7.30 to $9920.74; records of his blood pressure and heart rate, 110/72 at age thirty-five, 119/76 at age forty-three; business cards when he was chief draftsman at Douglas Aircraft Company, vice president at Doak Aircraft Company; a small newspaper clipping from a 1936 *Tulsa World* newspaper describing "staff changes" at the Spartan Aircraft Company "following the resignation of James B. Ford, chief engineer."

But mostly the box contained letters. More than a dozen sheets of yellowed onionskin paper filled with writing in sepia ink, dated between 1914 and 1921. They are from Henry Benjamin Ford to James Benjamin Ford, my great grandfather to my grandfather, from Jamaica to the United States. Apparently, James followed his mother and siblings to the United States a few years after they left, and his father wrote to him regularly. Each letter began upbeat, discussing the weather, mentioning some old friends who stopped by. Then Henry would move on to describing the progress of one of his ongoing schemes and inventions. There was the refrigeration system, a proposal he'd sent to the British government to help it with its military effort, the physical specifications and limitations of a human-powered plane he was developing, the Velontopede. In one, he wondered

116

if there might not be a good business to be had in the export of Panama hats.

Then almost every letter veered off in sudden fits of self-recrimination and doubt. Henry pined for his son and missing family. He lamented his financial insolvency. He expressed regrets about his failures and that he had nothing to leave his son other than the work he started and had been unable to finish.

In an early letter, there was this:

I am sorry that you have learnt all the evil things about your mother and her people; it was a mistake to have anything to do with that class of people, but the mischief having been done, I endeavored to do the best I could for my children and to elevate their mother from her disgusting surroundings and connections and keep you all with as clean souls as I could; but it was not to be....

I read and was hungry for details, but there were no more. Who was this woman? What were the circumstances of her life? What guilt or secret or agony caused her to leave her husband in such pain? Yet, in spite of her treachery, in spite of his laments that she was turning the other children against him and not giving them the letters he wrote, he still asked James to take good care of her and his siblings.

The last letter I have of Henry's, written just before his death, show that he died penniless and without reconciling with his wife and other children. According to a fragment of another letter written to James, it's unclear by whom, Henry had spent his last years in a rather degraded way. In a distasteful tone, the writer said he or she regretted having to inform James that Henry was "living rather more intimately than necessary" with a woman who was his maid. "Colored, of course," the writer added.

There were no letters from James back to Henry. But there were many letters from James, after Henry's death, to various authorities. He was seeking a variety of official documents and records. In one case, he was trying to track down a legacy that might be owed to his mother. He was asking for birth and death records. And as I reviewed the documents my grandfather received and kept, I uncovered an unexpected chronology. A wedding certificate noted that Henry B. Ford, of age, widower, surgeon-dentist, and Rachel Gilks, of age, spinster, no rank or profession, were married at St. Andrews Church on the island of Guiana, on June 20, 1901. Henry was forty-eight; Rachel was thirty-two. Another document stated that an unnamed male child was born to Rachel Gilks on August 28, 1896. My grandfather's birthday. But five years before his parents were married. Assuming that Henry was, in fact, his father.

There was also a letter from a dentist in Utica, New York, inviting my grandfather to come for a holiday dinner. I had heard that my grandfather, after learning dentistry from his own father, had apprenticed himself to a dentist in the States, finished high school, and then worked his way through the Massachusetts Institute of Technology. I called the Utica, New York, school district. A harried secretary became suddenly attentive and interested when I told her what I was looking for. Within a week, a high school transcript for James Ford appeared in my mailbox. Tears sprang to my eyes when I saw that under address and parent's name, someone had written the lonely letters, "Y.M.C.A." Not surprisingly, he did best in math and science and less well in the softer subjects. I called the MIT alumni office. The secretary there was accustomed to such inquiries; she even invited me to visit. I learned James had studied naval architecture and marine engineering and wrote a thesis on "The Design and Construction of an Aerodynamic Balance with Six Degrees of Freedom." Somehow this shook loose other memories of my grandmother telling me how James—or Jim, as she called him—had put himself through college, eating the same meal at a local diner over and over again because it was the cheapest he could find.

I too had put myself through my last three years of college with only very limited and erratic assistance from my grandmother and father on those rare occasions when I was financially desperate. I too had tried to find ways to eat, and to do most other things, as cheaply as possible. But beyond our similarities, what was most revelatory about this information about my grandfather was how much it explained his behavior toward my mother. Clearly, he had tried to make up for his own childhood deprivations by showering his daughter with lessons and contests and education. He had pushed her to make the most of every opportunity he dangled in front of her. And when she balked, he hit her. At least once that she was willing to discuss. Who knows how many other times she refused to mention. His rages were inexcusable but also, finally, understandable. As was her rebellion.

* * *

The enigma of Rachel, Henry's wife, deeply interested Linda and me. Linda knew Henry did not father Rachel's eldest daughter; however, Rachel's wedding certificate listed her as a "spinster," not a divorcee or widow, and Henry as a "widower." She had five more children with Henry, and by listing out the rough dates of their births, Linda and I discovered two or three were born before they were married. We tried to imagine how an educated, worldly, well-traveled, older man ended up with a woman from "disgusting surroundings." We wondered if Rachel was a domestic at the home of some friend of Henry's. Or perhaps a prostitute. There was no answer and no one to ask.

Linda discovered we were distantly related to a former diplomat and vice president of Panama, Guillermo Ford, who once appeared splashed over the news headlines covered in the blood of his bodyguard when he survived an assassination attempt. Linda also had a letter from my grandmother to Linda's parents. In it, she said that she'd already shared everything she knew about the family and added, "I never heard anything about the kidnapping." Kidnapping? Again, there is no one to ask for clarification.

In 1910, an uneducated woman with no money or means of support somehow got five children onto a steamer from Jamaica to the United States without her husband's company or knowledge. Linda and I had both heard the rationalization that it was done so the children could be educated; but Linda pointed out that Rachel raised the children on a seamstress's salary, moving from apartment to apartment to skip out on irate landlords to whom she owed back rent, and that all the children did poorly at school. My grandfather, the one left behind, was the only one of his siblings to attend college.

I have photographs of Henry and Rachel. Singly, not together. Henry's is a head shot, showing him to be handsome and well-groomed, bearded, with a broad face and somewhat squashed nose. There is something distinguished and devilish in his face, even though his expression is serious. In Rachel's photo, she is also serious, but out of preoccupation more than thoughtfulness, it seems. Her mouth is stiff with what appears to be the unfamiliar effort of smiling. She wears a Victorian dress and no jewelry other than a wedding band, and she is not especially pretty. Her

hands appear strong, with well-muscled backs and fingers. It occurred to me that those were hands accustomed to hard work,
not the hands of a gentlewoman. There were rumors that she may
have been mulatto, and a vague shadow does play about her face.
What I saw most in her face was my grandfather's. They shared
the same proud nose, suspicious eyes.

Linda gave me a copy of Rachel's death certificate. Age, 75
years, 10 months, 9 days. Trade, housewife. Address, the Bronx.
Marital status, widow. Citizenship, English. Birthplace, British
West Indies. Cause of death, adenocarcinoma of uterus metasta-
sis to lungs. Date of birth, September 30, 1869. The same as mine.
And my uncle.

In all those many times that my grandfather mentioned the
coincidence of his son and granddaughter being born on the
same day, he never mentioned that his mother shared our birthday. Why would he not have added her name to the list? Shame
is the only answer I came up with. Shame he saw echoed in his
daughter's own bad choices and perhaps even worse behavior.

Uncovering all this information was like walking into an
emotional spiderweb—I felt the soft stickiness of the invisible
threads of this ragged past against my skin but could not see exactly where the strands had landed. I wiped at my face, not quite
ready to accept this strange, shared legacy, but the traces of the
web remained.

* * *

In another black-and-white photograph, my mother, a pretty
young girl of six, stands, smiling confidently, her legs spread into
a sturdy V, her hands clasped behind her back, dressed for an occasion, hair curled, dress and matching hat set at a jaunty angle,

a big bow tied under her chin and wearing short socks and black buckle shoes, typical 1930s style. The sun is strong on one side of her face and casts dramatic black shadows behind her. Behind her is an airplane. It seems that the photographer meant to take a picture of both the girl and the plane, but enchanted by her beauty, or perhaps suddenly more proud of his human than mechanical creation, focused in on the little girl instead. Only a tire and the underside of part of the wing and nose of the plane are visible. The contrasts are high. The plane is shiny and reflective, gleaming in the bright light.

For most of my life, when I looked at this picture, I saw only the girl. I would look at the youthful innocence on her young face and wonder why there were no echoes of it in the face of my mother. I wondered if, sharing her features, I would share her fate. At some point, when I was in my mid-thirties, I looked beyond the little girl to the plane. This was the 1936 Spartan Executive, the first all-metal aircraft, the plane I was told my grandfather never got credit for designing.

All my life, I had my doubts; was this just another apocryphal story from the unreliable narrator who was my mother? Now, I could find out: aviation history, so tied to military and political history, is well documented. I searched the Internet and uncovered a book with a gold cover and the headline *The Spartan Story* splayed across it in maroon. There were detailed descriptions about the development, engineering, manufacturing, and features of all the planes made by the Spartan Aircraft Company. The chapter on the Spartan Executive begins:

The Spartan Executive was a true aviation legend. From an unlikely beginning in a small, Midwestern factory during the depths of the Great Depression, it was destined

122

to become one of the most highly regarded planes of that era. Built to the luxurious tastes of the rich oil "executives," it rivaled in comfort the most opulent limousines of the day. In performance, it was second to none, cruising at a remarkable 200 miles an hour and with a range of over one thousand miles.... For years, "Major" Ed Hudlow had dreamed of building a really superior plane, one that used state-of-the-art technology and would exceed all other private planes in speed, comfort, and safety.... The first step in the execution of this plan was the hiring of a competent design engineer. After several interviews, James B. Ford was selected. A 39-year-old aircraft industry veteran, Ford had been designing planes since 1919. He started work on the Executive in January of 1935... and had the practically hand-built plane completed by March of the next year, 1936.

As I read these words, I felt a hardened spot of distrust inside me begin to dissolve. Both for my mother and her father. The Spartan Executive was considered a groundbreaking achievement, one of the first planes designed for the comfort of passengers, specifically oil executives. The Spartan Executive was made of gleaming, polished aluminum, its cockpit lavishly appointed with wood, leather, and upholstered seats, complete with ashtrays and magazine holders. It had a powerful engine and retractable landing gear, and it was a pleasure to fly. King Ghazi of Iraq had a Spartan made for his personal use, with his coat of arms woven into the upholstery and painted on the fin and his royal crown painted on the doors. This plane was designated the Eagle of Iraq.

I contacted the book's author and asked if he had more information about my grandfather. He had only one anecdote to share, which he said he believed but could not corroborate and so could not print: my grandfather was paid two hundred dollars a month to design this plane. After it had its first successful test flight, he asked for a raise to two hundred fifty dollars. He was not only told no, but because the plane was flying, they said his services were no longer needed. He didn't "resign"; he was fired. I felt a stab of long-deferred pain for him.

The author also told me that the Spartan Executive represented an incredible legacy, one of which I could be proud. Proud. This was not a feeling I had often associated with my mother or her parents. I had for so long discarded so many things from my past; the Spartan gave me something I could hold up, hold onto.

I took the author's comments as a welcome instruction and tried to make room in my heart for this new emotion. These new feelings made me want more. I asked if he knew where I might see one of these beautiful planes. I expected him to direct me to a museum, but he said that of the thirty-four planes originally made, many are still flying, and that the Spartan Executive was considered one of the most valuable and collectable of vintage planes. He said it was simple to track down owners on the Federal Aviation Administration registry.

He also sent me a link to a Web site where a Spartan was for sale. Photographs of this fully restored plane show its polished aluminum exterior glinting in the bright sunshine as the plane banks over the rolling green hills and farmland of California's central valley. An ocher yellow Spartan emblem of a helmeted warrior was painted by the tail. In 1937, this plane sold for twenty-two thousand dollars, five thousand more than its closest competitor did. Sixty years later, sellers were asking more than three hundred thousand dollars for the plane that my grandfather had been paid a couple thousand dollars to design. Reading all this,

I wished he could have known. I wished my great grandfather could have seen that his son did take the lessons learned at the feet of his father and invented something complete and whole. And valuable. That out of the bits and pieces and fragments of possibilities that were my grandfather's early life, he had created something that not only worked but also became a part of history.

I got on the FAA registry and found the name of an owner who lived just a few hours away from me. I called cold, stumbled over my words when a woman picked up the phone, trying to explain who I was and what I was hoping for. She was skeptical at first, taking me for some kind of a solicitor. But once she understood, this soft-spoken, gentle-sounding woman became all warmth and interest. She said that her husband had fully restored the plane to its original condition and would be delighted to show it to me. She added that they'd also be delighted to meet me. Simply, I understood, because I was the granddaughter of the plane's original engineer. Pride again, that strange new emotion, rose up in me.

I drove for hours down a winding, wooded road on a damp, dreary day. My eyes filled with tears from time to time, which spilled over and dried and then spilled again as I thought of that old man with his pencils in the laundry room and the little girl who wondered what he was doing. I wondered if it would matter to him that the granddaughter who was "no bother" was now bothering to uncover his life, his legacy. I wondered if it would make up for anything that came before or after.

I headed into a remote and rural corner of northwest Connecticut, past a gun shop, down a dirt road, and onto a bumpy driveway that edged a grass airstrip defined by a line of woods and a row of low buildings, many open on one side. I went into the largest of the buildings and was greeted by a man who showed me to a table where he had spread books, papers, and other documents related to my grandfather's plane. He had personally restored the plane I was about to see. Other men peered out at me from under the wings or behind the engines of planes they were disassembling or putting back together, their shy, interested smiles crinkling the skin around their eyes. Owners of the Spartan Executive arrived and added a briefcase full of other yellowed papers to the pile on the table. I had brought my binder of yellowed letters. We thumbed through one another's paperwork, and I read them the passage where my great grandfather discussed the energy and lift needed to get his human-powered flying machine, the Velontopede, off the ground.

A mechanic looked at me quizzically, asked for the date of the letter, and said, "The things he's writing about, the things he's trying...they're decades ahead of their time."

I laughed with surprise and relief. "So, he wasn't just a crazy old man?" I said.

The mechanic shook his head. Not at all.

We left the warmth of the cavernous garage and walked through the dissipated rain and a soggy field to an open hangar where the plane sat, incongruously shiny in the dull day. The men admitted that they'd polished it for me. I let their pride wash over me, still unused as I was to my own. I walked around the plane and looked beneath the fuselage at the first retractable landing gear ever made. They opened the door and suggested I step inside. I sat in the back, where there were two comfortably upholstered passenger seats with ample legroom, magazine racks, and ashtrays. A jump seat had been ingeniously designed to fold out of the armrests between the two seats. I leaned into the cockpit. The dashboard was black with white letters on the elegantly simple gauges. The steering wheel was wood. They said it was all original, other than the one regulatory concession to modern aviation controls, a federally mandated transponder that they had tucked tidily under the dashboard.

The owner told me the plane was a pure pleasure to fly, full of spirit, power, and grace. I heard those words and thought how close my grandfather and my mother had come to embodying those qualities themselves; and how they both let those qualities become shadowed by bitterness instead.

The plane did not go up in the wintertime, so there would be no flying that day. But that didn't matter to me. I came to see the object. I came to see something of the man who had created it. We walked back to the main hangar, and the mechanics showed me an elegant coffee-table book about vintage airplanes. They flipped to a section toward the back and showed me pages that profiled the plane I'd just seen.

"It's for you," they said. "The book. We'd like you to have it."

I had nothing for them, I protested. They shook their heads. They were just happy to have met me. The fact of my having come, three generations later, was more than enough.

I wondered if it would have been enough for my grandfather, if my interest could have been some consolation for the other insults of his life. I wondered if, had he lived long enough to see his creation become a part of history, it would have soothed his rage, his disappointment. I wondered if, had he seen how many of his qualities—his stubbornness, drive, independence, resourcefulness, seriousness—has been passed down to his granddaughter, it would have softened his scowl. It was too late for him to take any pleasure in what I had become, but it wasn't too late for me to feel pride for at least some of what he had been.

Daisy

When Jason and I were about nine and ten years old, our mother moved us a few blocks up the street from the Fairfax house to a white-stucco, red-tile roofed home at the base of Hollywood Hills. As young as we were, we had questioned each other already about why Mom didn't work, how Mom supported us. We suspected, hearing the clipped conversations, sensing our mother's need and our grandmother's resentment, that plenty of money flowed in a single direction from one woman to another and that Grandma Daisy had either bought or somehow enabled our mother to buy this house. But our mother never let this fact slip, never showed anything that resembled gratitude, and when Grandma bought a house just a few blocks from us, she was furious.

"That controlling bitch. She moved here just so she could spy on me."

In fact, Grandma rarely came to our new house, but because hers was on the way to school, my brother and I often went there. We started many mornings walking down the steep hill that flowed away from our cul-de-sac, waiting for the light at the large intersection with the arching streetlamps that marked where Laurel Canyon and Fairfax Avenue ended and Hollywood Boulevard began. We'd then head down the block to her cream-colored house with the white picket fence and the front yard filled with pink rosebushes and orange birds of paradise. We opened the small gate that barred the driveway and hemmed in her overactive terrier. We'd come up the back steps, over the small patio with two webbed chairs, through the den with her gray vinyl recliner and console color television, into the breakfast room, where her large, round table would already be set with dishes, silverware, and two tall glasses of orange juice she had squeezed just moments before.

At the table, we flipped through the paper or finished homework, while she cooked and hummed or sang snatches of songs she remembered from her childhood in Vermont. She started us off with oatmeal for my brother and Cream of Wheat for me, each bowl marked in the center with a dab of butter, a spill of milk, a swirl of maple syrup. Then she served plates of scrambled eggs with toast and bacon for Jason, sausage for me. This was followed by half a grapefruit with a sprinkle of brown sugar, each section carefully cut apart to make it easy for us to eat. Once we were done, we always tried to help her clean up, but she insisted she had all day to clean up after us. Then she shooed us out the front door while she stood among her flowers, blowing kisses off her fingertips and telling us to come back after school, that it would be quiet and we could do our homework, stay for dinner. Just yesterday, she'd bought some nice lamp chops on special, she'd bake us a potato, we could watch our shows on television, spend the night if we wanted to, she'd just changed the sheets on our beds.

I spent a lot of time at Grandma's house. I had my own room furnished with a king-size bed that seemed to swallow me in its firm and comfortable embrace. There was also a matching dressing table and bureau, white with gold trim and ornate drawer pulls, and gauzy curtains that let the sunshine in but blocked the bulk of the light from the tall streetlamp just outside. I sat at her kitchen table while she cleaned and chopped vegetables or sliced oranges or peeled potatoes or pored over coupons, and listened to her chatter. She'd found bargains last week at Ralph's where oranges were ten cents less a pound than at the Safeway; the interest rates at a new bank were a quarter percent higher than the bank she used, but she supposed the convenience of being able to walk to her bank was worth something, too; the gardener she'd just hired did a better job pruning the roses than the last guy, who was really no good but she felt sorry for him.

In all things, Grandma was a bargain hunter. She would drive five miles out of her way to save a few pennies per pound. She kept string in drawers, rubber bands in a ball, buttons in jars. She clipped coupons and used a small notebook and stub of a pencil to record every expenditure she made, including the dime she put into the parking meter. When she spent money, she pried her wallet open carefully, wet her thumb, crosshatched from the years of cutting vegetables, and counted out the individual bills, one by one, making sure none were sticking together.

Grandma, who was born in 1899 and so came of age during the Great Depression, described herself as "careful" with money; her daughter, who was born in 1930 and so came of age during the boom years following World War Two, said her mother "spent quarters to save nickels." Grandma said she'd grown up poor, but "We never noticed because we were happy." My mother, who'd grown up with abundance, kept track of every slight.

Grandma often told animated, funny, and cheerful tales of her long-gone family life. She described the river behind her childhood home where she and her sisters would go skating in the winter. She talked about the woman who lived down the street with four sons who were drinkers, but who considered herself lucky because they were never drunk at the same time. She bragged about taking a job at the general store downtown, where she was able to get an old woman who came in every week to poke around but never spent any money to make a purchase.

She told me that her mother was Welsh Protestant and her father was Irish Catholic, and they fought like crazy. He'd retreat to his family farm a few miles away for a while, "and then they'd make up just long enough to make another baby." She had four sisters, "and each of the Bolger girls was known for something special. One was the most musical, the other the sweetest, another was the smartest, the other the most capable, and oh dear, I was so happy and vain to have been called the most beautiful." In spite of her beauty, she was also proud to proclaim that she was the only Bolger girl who wasn't pregnant when she got married. Her own mother—"that would be your great grandmother," she'd say—"was a wonderful, sweet, musical woman who was not very practical and had a rebellious streak in her. She used to scandalize the neighbors by sewing on the porch on Sundays when you weren't supposed to be doing any work. Of course, she could have sewed inside, but she wanted everyone to see just what she was doing."

One of her favorite stories was about how a family fight resulted in her success in business. "One day when I was a baby," she said, "my father's sister—she had flaming red hair, and you know how hot-tempered redheads are—came to the house and said she was going to steal me and have me baptized. My mother refused and oh, they got in such a fight! My aunt gave my mother a black eye, ripped me from her arms, and took me to church. I cried and cried, but then the priest gave me a penny, and I quieted right down. I always say that's why I've been good in business ever since." All my grandmother's sisters—"they would be your great aunts"—were teachers. Grandma went to business school and worked in an office instead.

Eventually, she met James and got engaged. But she said she would not marry him until she'd paid off the mortgage on her mother's house. "I've been paying off other people's mortgages ever since," she'd always add. My grandmother was a hard-driving, hardworking real estate agent and investor who marked the progress of her life as a series of houses, those she'd bought and sold, those she made a lot of money on, those that had earned less, those she'd bought for her son, her daughter, and then one for Owen to live in, just down the block. There was the mobile home park she wished she'd held onto. The view from the house where we spent so much time as children.

And always, the house in Redondo Beach. That beautiful house. Such a nice neighborhood. So many lovely families. Close to the beach. What wonderful times we had there when your mother was a child, she'd say, the energy leaving her voice.

Her lips would tighten, and she'd look off out the window.

"Your mother was such a beautiful child," she'd say. "Such a sweet, obedient, wonderful girl. Her art teacher said she was the most talented pupil she'd ever had. All her teachers said that about her."

The drawings in my grandmother's scrapbooks and the pictures on her wall corroborated her story. My mother had a sure hand as a young artist. She had an apple-cheeked face surrounded by blond curls and eyes open and innocent to the world in a way I'd never seen in photographs of myself at the same age.

Then my grandmother would mutter something about drink. If only my mother would stop drinking.

Or she might say, "We gave her every advantage."

Then she might add, "I guess we spoiled her."

Sometimes, even more quietly, "I suppose Jim pushed her too hard."

And then back to the drinking. "I wish there was something I could do to make her stop drinking."

But in her relationships, my grandmother had only two tools: food and money. Food she gave generously, and yet my mother always complained that she was "shoving food down our throats all the time." Money was given with more reluctance, more judgment, disapproval, ambivalence. After all, she had invested in her two children, and they made little of themselves in return. She gave them her husband's inheritance and then watched them squander it. She bought them homes in which she was then not welcomed.

* * *

When I was in my late twenties, my grandmother died quietly in her sleep. She was ninety-two years old and in general good health, suffering only the usual degradations to sight, hearing, mental agility, memory, and physical robustness that come with advanced age. She had a small heart attack, and the doctor told Jason that usually, with people of her age, within a few days or weeks, she would probably have another heart attack that would kill her. This is exactly what happened. Given how much she had endured during her life, it was amazing to me that her heart hadn't given way many years earlier.

In the years before she died, her movements became slow, but she was not overly frail; she was more absentminded, but not completely confused. Like my mother, my grandmother had always shown a blatant favoritism toward boys, but her bias softened in her later years, and we spoke regularly, at least every few weeks. Sometimes she called to tell me happy birthday, even though the date was months away. She was so embarrassed and confused the first time she made the mistake that I never again corrected her and simply thanked her profusely for her good wishes. Usually, after a few pleasantries, she simply skipped back through time to her childhood memories. She could still quote the Shakespeare she had learned in grade school, tell the stories I had heard innumerable times, and sing the flirtatious, humorous songs she had heard as a young woman.

"Daisy, Daisy, tell me your answer true," she'd sing in her age-roughened voice. "I'm half crazy for being in love with you!"

Coincidentally, I was living in Vermont then, having moved there after meeting the man who became my first husband, and Grandma repeatedly told me that she would love to come back, that she loved the green hills but was afraid the cold would be too much for her.

When she died, Jason, as he had done with our mother, took care of her affairs. There was no service for her because there was no one to come. She had outlived her four sisters, her husband, and both her children. Her fierce independence and inherent competitiveness had precluded having friends. She didn't have many material things of any value. She had already given me the gold bead and pearl necklaces with matching earrings and the box with the complete silver setting. My brother sent me a small rocking chair and gate-leg table that had been in my grandmother's childhood home and that she always said she wanted me to have so the pieces would return to Vermont.

Jason also sent me a couple boxes of photographs. Some I'd seen before, but some were new to me. There were pictures of my grandmother as a young woman on a large pinto horse, sitting in a park not far from where I now lived; another of her and her sisters gathered around a piano. There was a photo of my mother in her twenties, her hair a black fringe around her forehead and cheeks, her face dramatically made up, her expression simultaneously placid, focused, and serious. There was a photograph of my grandmother, hair short and waved around her face, a beaded dress hanging from her slender shoulders, her expression the same as my mother's. There was also a photograph of my grandmother's mother when she was in her twenties, and again, the expression on her face was remarkably similar to her daughter's and granddaughter's. On the back of this photo, my grandmother had written, "Anne Laura, or Annie Laurie."

I had not known that my mother was named after her grandmother or that I carried both her names, in reverse, within my own. All the things, I thought, that I didn't know, that I hadn't known to ask, about these women; all the ways that I didn't recognize what parts of them I carried within me.

I put the photographs of the three women next to one another and regarded them together. Each woman was beautiful in a way that was strong rather than soft. They had prominent noses and wide mouths, which I did not. They had strong jawlines and broad brows, which I did. They all also had the same dance of light and dark around their large, alert, challenging eyes. My great grandmother's eyes were pensive, my grandmother's eyes had a bit of mischief about them, and my mother's eyes brightened with a coy and knowing intensity. Each woman was unique yet carried the stamp of the other. I considered getting a photo of myself and adding it to the lineup. But I was afraid. I didn't want to find in my own eyes those things I'd rejected in theirs. I didn't want to set my face so close to theirs.

I turned away. And as I did, I was suddenly faced with my own face staring back at me from a mirror on the opposite wall. I froze, taken aback by seeing myself with the clarity of unexpected exposure. But I didn't turn away. I stared long and unashamedly into my features, now, in spite of my fears, appearing reflected next to theirs. I saw some things that were easy to identify: my father in the area around my mouth, my grandmother in the color of my hair, my mother in the squareness of my jaw. But the character of my own eyes eluded me. Looking into them was like staring down the long shaft of an old well and trying to identify the water from the surrounding darkness.

I wondered: if I claimed the intensity that was in these other women's eyes, would I have to own their other qualities, too? These women I had tried to leave behind, who stared at me now from beyond the grave, challenged me not only to accept what I found in their faces but also to see it in my own. I turned away from the mirror. I wasn't ready. But I was close enough that I put their photos in frames and lined them up on my bureau. So I could be reminded. So they'd be there when I *was* ready.

* * *

In the years before she died, my grandmother had told my brother and me repeatedly that she had taken care of all her affairs. She said she had everything settled because she did not want us to do for her what she had had to do for others. But there were many details that had apparently unraveled or been left undone, one of which was where she would be laid to rest. She had purchased a burial plot for herself next to her husband, but she had used this for my mother instead. She had purchased another, but it was up over the hill, isolated, alone. My brother and I both detested the idea of a coffin, so he had her cremated. Her ashes sat in a funeral home while we tried to decide what to do with them. Jason suggested sending them to me.

"She had so many happy memories of Vermont," he said. "And she kept talking about wanting to move back there. Maybe that's where she should go."

It was the season of slow decay and quiet death in Vermont, the season I had come to know and love as a quiet refuge from the other seasons of the year, one of the seasons that had been absent from my childhood. As we discussed our options, I looked out the window at all the living things that were fading and blazing in their death throes and wondered what I would do with the ashes if he sent them. I thought of the stories she had told me about her ancestral home, which I thought was still there, owned and lived in perhaps by one of my grandmother's nieces or cousins or some other relation. Was this where the ashes should go? In the river out back, perhaps?

We had been to her childhood home once before. Jason and I had been visiting our father in New Jersey; we must have been about seven or eight years old, and our grandmother's sister—a sweet spinster schoolteacher who had lived in the family home— had recently died. Grandma was coming to take care of her affairs and had asked our father to send us to her. He put us on a bus. My brother and I stared out the windows for the many-hour drive. We watched the daylight fade from the sky, silently wondering when the ride would end, how we would know when to get off, and wondering why, at stop after stop, everyone else was exiting the bus but no one was getting on, eventually leaving us as the only passengers.

Finally, sometime after dark, we pulled into a parking lot and the driver turned and grunted at us. Grandma was standing outside a dimly lit and deserted bus station with a drab coffee shop near an empty highway. I remember that it was cold and that our clothing was not warm enough. We had another long drive in the dark to the house where she had grown up. I was disappointed; the house was small, set close to the road, and hemmed in by a big boulder on the opposite side of the street. The rooms were dark and antiquated. The lighting was inadequate and florescent. My grandmother gave us a late supper, and we climbed the steep, narrow stairs to an unfamiliar bed.

The next day, she showed us the stream out back that had been the subject of so many of her stories. I expected to find a somnolent river with deep pools for swimming and broad expanses for skating. Instead, it was a noisy trickle of water over stones, nearly hidden by steep banks and overhanging brush. She had talked with grave respect about the slate quarries that took what small savings her father had made as a farmer when he loaned it to a relative who failed in this business that had made other men rich. All I saw were huge piles of gray rock shards and rubble. Even the weather was gray; the sun seemed tired, the clouds hung just above the old, dilapidated buildings. She took us to buy more appropriate clothes—mittens and boots—at a store staffed by a solitary, grizzled old man who did not smile.

Remembering the difference between my grandmother's stories and my memories, I wondered what could possibly be left behind now. My own experiences didn't help. I had been living in her state of green hills and gray weather for several years, and although I had learned to appreciate its rough beauty and occasionally I found my way through the chill countenance of its people and enjoyed the dramatic changes of the seasons, I never found the passion for the place that my grandmother had. I looked for what she had described so many times, and although I saw it with my eyes, I didn't feel it in my heart. What kind of a burial would there be for her here?

Eventually, for lack of a logical alternative, Jason had her ashes buried alongside her husband and daughter. And strangely, I went to her childhood home anyway. A photograph compelled me. It was hanging in the stairway of my old farmhouse. I was walking down my own set of steep, narrow stairs, having just come up on some small errand, when I stopped, each foot on a different step, and gazed into the picture. A cluster of people gathered on a low porch in front of tall windows shuttered in black and hung with white lacy curtains. The edge of some ornate wood trim was barely visible on either side of the porch columns. The back end of a Model T Ford jutted into the right side of the frame. An old woman with white hair swept into a bun sat in a rocker surveying the scene. She was surrounded by three young women sitting on chairs or the open porch edge and three young children standing in the yard as if they had just been called away from a game. A teenage boy stood near a window, his sleeves rolled up over his elbows, his thick black hair shorn close to the sides of his head. The women were each looking at something in their hands. The young man was the only one looking out at the photographer. The photo was casual, unposed, as if it were a warm-up, a precursor for a more formal photo about to be taken.

My great grandmother was the woman in the rocking chair. My great aunts were the women sitting in the other two chairs. My grandmother was the woman sitting on the edge of the porch in a white sundress with ties at the shoulders, her hair up in a net. My mother was the little blond girl in the yard, tugging on a strand of hair, much as I did and still do. They were both turned away from the photographer. From me. Suddenly, I wanted so much to see their faces. My grandmother had been a woman surrounded by a thin veil of sadness about how the lives of her children had turned out. This veil was punctuated only when she spoke of her own childhood in the house shown in the photo. Suddenly, I wanted to add something more to my memories of my grandmother; I wanted to see where she'd been happy.

So I got in my car and drove. The path was familiar. I used to drive it all the time when I was dating, long distance, the man whom I'd married a few years earlier, just shy of my twenty-fifth birthday. But back then, my travels had skirted the town where my grandmother had been born. Back then, I always turned north, I was always in a hurry, never took the time to take the short detour to see where she had grown up. After an hour of driving, road signs appeared to mark my progress, twenty-seven miles, twenty-two miles, sixteen miles, five miles to the town where she had been born. The same scenery fringed the two-lane road along its entire length: farms, cows, scrubby woodlands, open fields, rolling hills, the stubble of cut corn. At the outskirts of her town, I passed a small grocery store, a mobile home park, a VFW post, a discount beverage store. I came to a large and gracious town green lined with big brick buildings, solid, but with decay fraying their edges. At street level, there was a used clothing shop, a pizza parlor, a video rental place. Printed sheets or torn shades covered the windows above.

I didn't know where I was going. But once, when we were talking about her childhood, I had asked my grandmother the address of her family home.

"Forty-six River Street," she had said with joy at being able to recall this small fact, some eighty or more years later.

I had repeated the address over and over in my mind as if cramming for some test I thought I might someday be asked to take. It was still with me. And as I left the town green, the road sloped down toward a bridge and some railroad tracks, and I thought, a river is always at the bottom of a hill. I turned onto an unmarked road just before the bridge, and then a sign jumped into view: River Street. I looked for the river, but it was too small, hidden by its own banks, far below the road. I drove past a butcher, a few homes in need of upkeep, and looked not for her house but for the outcropping of rock I remembered from my childhood visit. There it was, sticking out from a curve in the road, a half mile or so down. Just beyond, on the opposite side, was a tiny, white farmhouse. I pulled over on the narrow shoulder. I stayed in the car. I felt like a teenager wandering through the bedroom of someone I was baby-sitting for. I didn't know what I was going to see, what I was hoping to uncover. And I didn't want to be caught looking.

I wondered for a moment if this was really the house. It was smaller than I remembered, even as I tried to correct for the years in between. But this had to be it. The street numbers had changed, but its location was correct. Unlike the other farmhouses I'd passed, this one had clearly been updated, maintained. It was quaint, with some of its original Victorian character. Instead of the unpainted siding and black shutters in the photograph, this house was vinyl sided in white with baby blue shutters. Lacy curtains, like those in the photo, hung in the windows, but the porch was gone. A sunroom had been added to the side of the house where open fields had been visible in the picture. Woods obscured that view now. There were modest gardens, a tidy lawn, and a huge pine tree where the Model T in the picture had been.

The front door was open. I hoped no one would come through it. I knew that I could get out, call hello, tell whoever appeared that my grandmother had grown up here, that I was passing by and was wondering how the house looked now. A woman had done just that to me at my old farmhouse not too long ago, and I had been thrilled to show her in. But that person was a stranger, and I might run into a distant relative here. I might have to start sharing stories and telling watered-down versions of unpleasant news. I might have to endure sympathy about the variety and nature of my familial "losses." I didn't want to have to try to summon up some emotion that seemed appropriate to this occasion but would have felt false to my actual experience.

So I sat in my car and I tried to picture my grandmother here as a young girl playing in the yard, cavorting with her sisters, taking her children back to visit their aunts and cousins in the summertime. None of these women was the woman I knew, but I tried to see her here. I heard her voice telling me about how happy her childhood had been. But I also heard the echo of other things she'd said or intimated. My great grandmother was sweet but impractical; she played piano but couldn't or wouldn't pay her bills; she had an unhappy, stormy marriage, and her in-laws hated her. I thought how much my great grandmother sounded like my mother.

Then, I thought of my grandmother's drive to go to business school, to get a good job, to marry an ambitious man. As much as she said she loved her early life, she had goals and dreams that took her, and then kept her, far away from here. She worked so hard, so assiduously to keep the poverty she said hadn't mattered to her at bay. She achieved much but never lost the fearful, parsimonious edge that kept joy away. It was this edge that my mother hated, railed and rebelled against. It was this grim determination, I realized, not joy, that must have fueled my grandmother's efforts to give her children so much. She must have pushed my mother with the same grinding, stubborn focus that had allowed her to pile up her pennies; in my mother's case, she piled up lessons, activities, contests.

If I was to believe the stories and the evidence, my great grandmother had been frivolous but also beloved. My grandmother was practical, respected for her ambition and hard work, and not liked so much as placated and cajoled for her money and the power money gave her over others who had less and wanted more. My mother was creative and irresponsible, and she alternately attracted and repulsed people, often with equal passion. And so I had to ask myself, what about me? I had watched these women from a cool and observant distance, doing the math, calculating what each had gained and lost by holding so stubbornly to those few tools that had served them well once or twice. No matter how their world was changing, how clumsy these implements proved to be when faced with new problems and new circumstances, they seemed unable to try their hand with new instruments or devices. Contrariness to expectations was perhaps what united them most.

I too had been contrary. I had defined myself primarily in opposition to these women, especially my mother. Sitting there in that car, staring at that farmhouse, I realized that I had tried to cherry-pick what these women had made of their own lives and had taken bits and pieces of what seemed most worthwhile. I worked in marketing and corporate communications, a profession that was both creative and pragmatic, taking a piece from each of them. I worked hard but allowed myself moments of indulgence, playfulness, revelry. I had been called both blunt and diplomatic with equal frequency. I tended toward seriousness but was also known for the creativity of my cooking, the comfort of my home, the energy of my parties, the intensity of my laugh. From time to time and in the right company, I could be downright silly.

I had traveled thousands of miles to escape these women but ended up landing on the shores of my grandmother's youth. I had tried to make a deal with my past, with my inheritance, and tease out only select parts from the uglier, clinging, cloying bits. I was almost thirty years old. The time for parsing and bargaining might now be over. It wasn't just that these women were dead; it was that they seemed to write their own life stories only in opposition to the generations that came before them. I had tried to do the same and had consistently found the effort unsatisfying. There was a reason, I was beginning to realize, why I was continually compelled to dig for the more complex, nuanced layers to the life stories they had given me. Yes, I wanted to add dimension to the characters they were. But in so doing, I was also looking for ways to add dimension to myself. It was time to stop looking only for what I should avoid in them and to start looking for what they had given me.

Decline

I don't know how my mother filled her days during the years we lived on Hillside Avenue in the early 1970s, when I was nine, ten, eleven years old. She didn't have a job. She didn't have work. One day I found her tugging at some pastel-patterned chiffon hanging from a dress form, her mouth pursed in agitation as she tried to get the bias-cut segments of the skirt to hang properly. Someone commissioned her to create a dress. But there was no joy or satisfaction in the task. She seemed pained by it. And the effort was never repeated.

Sometimes she said she was looking for a job. But only as a reason for not doing something else. Like the laundry.

"I can't be bothered with mundane tasks like dirty clothes!" she'd scream if I asked to be taken to the Laundromat. I filled the

145

tub with water, washed my clothes with a bar of soap, wrung them out by hand, and hung them on towel racks to dry.

"I can't be bothered with stupid errands like getting hydrogen peroxide," she said, indignant, when I asked her to fill a prescription from the doctor who had stitched my lip back to my lower gum after a fall from the jungle gym had split them apart. I collected my change and walked down to the Thrifty drugstore five blocks away.

She complained about money, about children who required the spending of it, about not having enough of it, about fathers who didn't send any, about mothers who wouldn't give her any, about friends who didn't contribute any. One day I collected all the change and small bills I had earned from odd jobs and baby-sitting, put it in an envelope, and left it on her desk chair. I scrawled a note saying that I knew it wasn't much, but I hoped it helped. In a rare moment of tenderness, she gave it back to me and told me not to worry, that this was her problem, not mine. I understood that but didn't believe it was a problem she could, or would, solve on her own.

For me, I spent the daytime hours in the welcome safety, structure, and reward of school. Which, quite simply, saved me. The young women who were my grade school teachers wore simple shifts, wrote clear instructions, and meted out judicious rewards for both effort and accomplishments. They told my mother and me that I was a pleasure to have in class, that I was always helpful to other students, that I was "gifted" intellectually, but that I was intensely shy, especially about physical activities. My terror about playground time was a small price to pay for the reward of a smile from Miss Siegel or Miss Bernstein when I gained another point for reading yet another book, or handed in a tidy homework assignment, or wrote a poem they found worthy of hanging on the wall, or moved quickly from one color to the next in the supplemental SRA extra-credit literacy program, or used my study time to tutor another student.

The Hillside house was where I had my first boyfriend, my first experience of being adored. We were in sixth grade. His hair and skin were the color of a brick, faded brown warmed with hints of red. The tips of his short, unkempt Afro were lightened blond by the California sun. He had slender fingers that moved when he talked, medium brown eyes, and one front tooth that slipped over the other like a lazily crossed leg. His smile was shyly flirtatious, his clothes managed to be both hip and ratty, he lived with his older brother and single mother in an apartment near our school, and he told me he had all kinds of blood mixed up inside him, a little bit of black, Chicano, white, and maybe some other things, too. He could ride his bike holding a wheelie for more blocks than any other kid at Gardner Street Elementary School could, and all the girls had crushes on him, but he didn't seem to know or care. He was an average student and had been kept back a grade once before, but he charmed our teachers with his dutiful attitude and gentle humor and gained status as one of the coolest kids in the school by having a disposition that was sweet in a slow, melting kind of way. He said he liked me not just because he thought I was pretty but also because he thought I was smart. When our teacher pulled me aside to help tutor other kids, he slung his eyes over toward our corner, a little jealous, a little protective.

Once or twice a week he would walk me home, carrying my books over the long blocks of Hollywood Boulevard that stretched more than a mile away from school, away from the direction of his own home. Sometimes we stopped and visited a friend who lived several blocks up a steep hill on a side street we passed on our way to my house. She had a mother who kept the kitchen stocked with white bread, Oreo cookies, and packaged snacks, and a collection of records that included Joni Mitchell, Carly Simon, Carole King, and James Taylor. There was an empty lot nearby where he liked to make jumps and obstacle courses for his bike. Other times he would come into my house with me, pretending he was there to visit my brother. We didn't know what to call our attraction, our friendship. Our feelings were too new, too inexplicable. We didn't know how to claim one another.

He made my mother laugh. She always welcomed him with a hug, and when he said he had to go home, she asked him to stay, said he was so darling, so amusing.

"Can't," he'd say, smiling. "My mother's expecting me for dinner."

One day, he stopped me at the bottom of the long flight of red tile stairs that led up to my house. He said he couldn't stay, had to get home, but he wanted to ask me something before he left. He brushed my long, stringy blond hair back over my shoulders. My cheeks burned with the reflected heat of his seriousness.

He licked his lips, looked at the ground, then into my face, and said, "Can I kiss you good-bye?"

I think I nodded. Perhaps I managed a mumbled yes, thoughts of the kiss crowding against worries that my mother might look out the window, see us, call to us, spoil the moment. But miraculously, it remained ours, and we tilted our heads toward one another. His lips were an instant of plush pressure against my own. A rush of warmth ran down my neck and into my arms and legs. He pulled back, smiled at me, then turned and walked away. I ran up the stairs feeling that I had just been given something precious, something I could call my own.

I wanted to tell my mother. She liked him; I allowed myself the thought that she might be happy for me. But caution won, and instead I asked her, feigning a casualness I didn't feel, what she would do if I ever had a black boyfriend.

"I would disown you."

Eventually, she found out or figured out that this boy was hanging around to see me, not my brother. When she told me what she knew, I cried, not sure whether I was going to lose her or him. She laughed at me. I reminded her of what she had said. She scoffed, saying I was silly and oversensitive.

But by this time, she saw him as hers, not mine. He was another charming young man who took the time to make her smile. She wasn't accepting him for me, but for herself.

* * *

However my mother spent her daytime hours, the evenings continued as they had a few years earlier on Fairfax Avenue, except the company began to change. Gone were the artists and actors. Now, we were increasingly surrounded by a strange amalgam of misfits, has-beens, and those trying to wriggle their way into film, music, or art.

Tommy, a weedy gay man, lived on one floor of a house covered in flowering vines behind the "country" store in the middle of Laurel Canyon. He had wisps of gray hair parted steeply along one side of his head and then pulled back into a slender stub of a ponytail that curled up on itself. He favored slouchy velvet hats, leather vests, and bi-colored shoes. Stutz Bearcat stopped by on his way to the pound with a stray dog; we begged and pleaded—successfully—to keep her. Tommy suggested we name her Spats, because of her white paws, but Owen called her "Shorty," and it stuck. Tommy's fingers shuddered slightly as he dragged on a slender, brown, filterless cigarette or the stub of a joint, and he squinted against the smoke, deepening the crow's feet around his eyes and the crescents on either side of his mouth. His laugh was sudden and rough, a tool scraping wood, followed by smoke drifting, incongruously lazy, from his nose and mouth.

Dane was a carpenter, a barrel of a man who wore blue jeans slung low under his battered leather belt and a white T-shirt snug against his large belly. His brown hair hung in a swath over his eyes, which, when he laughed or smiled, scrunched up shyly behind this sheer curtain. Dane's lap was a haven I sought regularly. Even though I was old enough to start to be interested in boys, I was still young enough to be looking for paternal comforts. His lap was where I ran to one Saturday afternoon when I stepped into my mother's bedroom and found her buried beneath a man I didn't know as a party raged on downstairs. Dane let me cry out my confusion, soak his shirt with my tears.

Claudia, who lived next door, was a moon-faced woman with skin the color of a chocolate bar. She had been a back-up singer for the Rolling Stones, the subject of the song "Brown Sugar." We would point to her name on the album cover and show our friends. But I never heard her sing, and her deep brown eyes were always clouded with sadness, disappointment, drugs, or sometimes all of these.

A strangely tall, somber Japanese photographer was making books about the United States and took pictures of us over several days on several different visits. One photograph showed my mother lounging in imitation of her once-youthful self on a love seat, wearing a floppy hat with a faux flower on the rim. Another showed all three of us collected on a piece of beat-up furniture like three things that had been blown together by the wind.

Cliff was a pencil-thin, delicately arranged, fey man, who dressed in striped pants and double-breasted jackets, smoked dark brown cigarettes, and had a frizz of hair that hung to his shoulders and a wrist that was perpetually limp.

There was Juan, someone my mother knew from the garment industry, who looked at her with the longing of an abandoned dog. He would sometimes walk with me to my room at night and tell me a story about a pond full of cheerful animals and a tadpole that saddened his friends by disappearing, only to return a few months later and surprise everyone with his new shape, his new voice, his impressive croaking. There was a torpid guy named John, who came from over in the Valley, a town called Reseda that she constantly mocked as suburban, boring, square.

Jason and I sometimes discussed the relative merits of these various men as replacement fathers. We thought Dane not quite up to the job because of his drinking. We approved of Juan, even through the confused dislocation of finding him in bed with her on a few occasions, because he was protective of her, frequently took her glass away from her instead of refilling it, and urged her to go to bed instead of having more. One night when strange noises awakened me, I found her, naked, soggy, muttering, and splayed across the extra bed in my brother's room; some young men, perhaps friends of his, were batting at her pendulous breasts and swollen stomach with toy paddles they'd found in the closet, as if she were something that had washed up on the beach. Juan came into the room and rescued her from this indignity by slinging her arm over his shoulder and dragging her down the hall, back to her own bed.

The parties no longer ended with people merely crashing in sleep onto the furniture or floor; they devolved into furniture crashing against furniture, glasses smashing into a wall, voices raised in twisted coils of anger. Sometimes I fought back with my own raised voice, standing at the top of the stairs, screaming against the waves of noise from below, gripping the metal railing, pleading with the adults to stop, to be quiet, my voice broken with sobs as I choked out again and again that I had to go to sleep, to get up early, to be at school in the morning. Please, please, please, I'd howl, stop shouting, shut up, shut up, shut up.

Sometimes the voices died down. Sometimes someone came to the bottom of the stairs and yelled back that I should shut my own fucking mouth, little stinking brat that I was, and go back to bed. Usually, nothing happened at all, my own voice too small to make any dent in the noise of my mother's life.

I was just enough older now that I fought against the increasing chaos of her world by finding ways to stay away from it. After school, my first line of defense was the library. I would go there, sit cross-legged among the dark stacks of books, and read. But that only gave me a couple of hours of escape before the frowning librarian would come around to shoo any remaining children outside and lock the doors behind us. From there, I wandered to my grandmother's house instead of home. She would encourage me to lie down on her golden, tufted sofa for a rest or to sit in her ample recliner in front of the television, my bare legs sticky against the vinyl, or to have a snack, or to stay for dinner, or to spend the night. I frequently did one or all of these things.

One day, an actress who lived down the street from us called out to me from the garden in her front yard when I was trudging up the hill. She invited me into her home, asked me to help with her new baby, took me with her family to Big Sur. She always left the door open for me to come in; to feed the gurgling, smiling infant; to participate in a craft or sewing project; to listen to John

Denver; or to just hang out and watch a much more peaceful domestic scene as it unfolded day after day.

And there were the Hollywood Hills, steep expanses of decomposed granite that ran away under my feet as I walked and climbed and discovered paths that meandered through the eucalyptus and jacaranda scrub. I would wander these hills for the long hours of the afternoon and weekends, finding hollows beneath trees where I would sit and dream about my escape from the disquiet at home by making elaborate plans for setting up a camp right there. My actress friend had given me a book called *Living on the Earth* that provided instructions about building a shelter, creating natural refrigeration, collecting plants and berries. I read its instructions carefully and plotted how infrequently I could visit home for food. I had already practiced my mother's signature enough to write whatever facsimile I needed for report cards. I could get a meal and shower at my grandmother's house. It never occurred to me that I would be missed—or, if I were missed, that anyone would care. I imagined only the relief someone would experience at the evaporation of my sad, serious, scrutinizing face.

But I kept going back. In spite of the quiet nights and full refrigerator at my grandmother's house, the bittersweet smelling baby and tousled rooms at the actress's house, I always felt the desire and need to see what was happening at my mother's house. And to see if there was anything I could do to manage the chaos, to keep the enterprise just above water. As I had always done, I picked up the dirty plates, washed the dishes, rearranged the pillows, organized my drawers, and scrubbed the tiles on the front porch on my hands and knees. I also found a way to be at home and away from home simultaneously. I holed up in my room at the end of the hallway and read. I checked out books from the library until it seemed I'd consumed everything on the shelves for kids my age range and several beyond. My father sent me horsey books from time to time—*Misty of Chincoteague, Black Beauty, Stormy*—and I read them over and over and over again, sometimes all at the same time, longing for someone to discover me, to see the soft beauty beneath my unkempt and protected exterior, to take me away from those who misunderstood me, and to care for me with patient caresses, soft salves, nourishing grains, and warm bedding.

But the books I cherished most were my mother's childhood copies of the *Heidi* series. Thick pages the color of weak tea were filled with bucolic descriptions and dreamy color plates of a cherubic blond girl cavorting among goats in the countryside and being tucked into a straw bed overlooking the hillsides by a laconic and protective grandfather who fed her hunks of cheese and bread. The stories filled my head with visions of what might be possible for me. But the books also contained a historical artifact of what was once possible for my mother. In the front of each volume, written in the formal script of a schoolteacher's hand, was this line: "To Anne, for perfect attendance at Sunday School." Sunday school. It was as foreign a place to me as the hillsides where Heidi grew up; it sounded equally pure and unspoiled. I would run my fingers over these words and imagine my mother as the beautiful child I had seen in the photographs on my grandmother's walls, her saucer eyes full of sensitivity and shyness now long gone. I would wonder at the idea of this younger, idealized, obedient, subservient version of her, of all she had lost, all she had given away.

I could not imagine how the child implied in that one short phrase grew up to become a Miss Redondo Beach, a model, and then a drunk. I could not imagine what kinds of things had happened to her in between her childhood Sundays at church and my personal present to turn her into the woman I knew. There was no way for me to picture, much less comprehend, the pressures her parents, their ambitions fueled by their own irresponsible parents and Depression-era privations, had put on her. I was too young even to consider the endless promises presented to a beautiful young woman in the postwar, bright-eyed, and wholesome fifties, and how these dreams could have been twisted in upon themselves in the alternate universe presented by the sixties and then the radical turnaround required by the sometimes-violent reactions, disappointments, and retrenchment of the seventies. All I knew was that I wanted desperately to be someone completely different from her. But this too was an effort in which she fought me.

My mother did have intermittent bursts of industry. They were usually directed at turning Jason or me into artists, musicians, or, even better, income-producing models or actors. She would decide that we must have art instruction and then sign us up for classes at Barnsdall Art Park. But she hated driving us there and picking us up, so we would finish out the session by taking the bus, and then there would be no more classes. She would suddenly find it unimaginable that we didn't play piano and would then trundle us to some small studio tucked into a street of warehouses, where an unattractive man with dandruff littering his shoulders would try to teach our fingers to obey his instructions on the keyboard; for a month or so, she would holler at us from time to time to "go practice." But she invariably became distracted, and so did we.

She rounded us up for the occasional casting call. I recall once trying desperately to summon up what I thought was the required, if completely insincere, internal intensity to camp it up with a sham smile for the directors going through their perfunctory motions, but the only thing that happened was they took a Polaroid of me and threw it on a round table among dozens of other photographs. She had some friends, a model and a photographer who had taken new names by turning their more traditional ones backward—Nerak had been Karen, Yendor had been Rodney. She wrote me a note to excuse me from school for a morning, saying I had a doctor's appointment, when in fact I was to spend a few hours making faces for Yendor's camera with Nerak's coaching. Another time she took me to the studio of a music photographer, Dorothy Tanous, where she had set some tattered theater seats underneath a skylight. We spread out the detritus of my mother's modeling days—dresses with beads falling off, bright boas that left feathers floating in the air, floppy hats with bent flowers on the brims—and in the darkened room, Dorothy stayed quiet and asked me to do nothing more than to dress up. The moody images she created seem to me still to capture the truest state of our lives at that time.

My mother lacked the disciplined energy and raw ambition her own mother had developed by growing up poor on that flinty farm in the cold-darkened hills of Vermont. All of her efforts on our behalf fizzled under her inevitable dissipation and my stubborn disinterest. Although her exhortations for me to go out and to use the good looks she insisted she gave me to make some money continued throughout her life, I learned quickly that she was no stage mother, and I was never going to be managed into some kind of child star. All I had to do was play along with her once-in-a-while bursts of activity. I understood in some inchoate way that her efforts to have me finish the work she had started would always be sabotaged by her native competitiveness and narcissism. In this, at least, we agreed: neither of us wanted me to be in the limelight.

Watching her on weekend mornings as she tried to work her mind and body out of the fog induced by the previous night's drinking was additional incentive to put no value in the variable stock of one's looks. She began her day by wrapping herself in a cheap, Asian-printed robe, gulping mugs of milk-whitened coffee and glasses of water, and then standing over the sink in her bathroom examining the shifting terrain of her once smooth-skinned, now red-blotched face. After she splashed her cheeks with water, she applied thick globs of some white cream that dissolved the dark shadows of yesterday's makeup. She squeezed witch hazel onto cotton balls and swiped at her face to remove the cream. She opened a different cosmetic pot and vigorously rubbed circles of some other cream into her ruddy skin. Then she examined the tabula rasa that was left behind, sticking out her chin to stretch and to tighten the jowls that were gathering in the distance, like some kind of threatening storm, tugging with irritation at the skin around her eyes—her signature feature, her point of pride—trying to smooth out the swelling pouches underneath, the creases at the edges. "Blue, gray, green eyes" she called them, recalling a favorite nickname of a long-forgotten boyfriend. "Blue, gray, green eyes," I silently repeated as I looked from my similarly colored eyes back to hers, two sets in the mirror, one gaining depth from the experience of life, the other fading away beneath age and abuse.

My mother's transformation began with the application of layers of mascara whisked from a fat pink tube onto her waiting eyelashes. Then she brushed an amalgam of soft blues, purples, and brown shadows into the crease of her eyes, drew a delicate slice of eyeliner along and out beyond the corners of her eyelids, slid a greasy magenta stick along her open-mouthed lips. I watched and wondered and knew that I never wanted to be that attached to my looks, that needful of whatever attentions they could bring me, that beholden to creating a face to present to the world. What I didn't realize was that this person fretting in front of the mirror was no more born to this role than I was. The twisting and squinting I saw in her face reflected not simply dissatisfaction with the insults of time and abuse she saw there but contortions inside her soul that were in a constant state of grating and sliding that would find release only in a regular spate of eruptions.

The fault lines appeared first as outbursts of hostility and paranoia toward visitors and neighbors. On a visit to see his former back-up singer next door, Mick Jagger had parked his Jaguar in front of our full-to-the-brim and never-used garage. I expected my mother to cajole and flirt with the famous rock and roller. Instead, she went into a rage at the supposed insult of his mis-parked car, screamed epithets at him, and insisted that if the offending vehicle were not removed immediately, she would have it towed or, worse, deface it herself.

Down the street from us lived an awkward teenager with a pudgy mother who had a little white dog that occasionally got loose and followed our dog Shorty to our house. My mother took a dislike to the yappy dog, the unattractive girl, her skittish mother. She said their dog shat in our yard. Which of course, Shorty and our other dog, a squat, dachshund mix named Rachel, did, too. Then one day her eyes lit up with a germ of an idea. She took a take-out Chinese food container from the garbage, filled it with a pile of dirt and dog shit, placed the white box into a lunch bag printed with yellow happy faces, and exhorted my brother and one of his friends to leave the bag on their doorstep, ring the bell, and run. The next day when I returned from school, my mother was laughed manically as she reported hearing about the woman's tears and disbelief when she opened the package and watched it spill all over her pristine, white, living room carpet.

Owen came by once, asking for keys to unlock a bicycle that he had kept at our house. Our mother not only refused but also taunted him with the keys. He reached out to grab them from her, and she fled down the hallway, Jason and I skittering ahead of her, trying to get out of the way. The argument ended when Owen put his fist through the window in my room and opened a deep gash in his forearm.

The mother of the famous fashion designer Rudi Gernreich lived in a deathly quiet house across the cul-de-sac. The sight of him, hand on his mother's elbow, escorting this feeble old woman to his car for a luncheon out, turned my mother's face dark with stormy anger.

She wandered from window to window, peering out at him, muttering, "He's a fucking misogynistic faggot. Fags have taken over the fashion industry. Who the hell does he think he is? I'm the better designer; I'm the one who is the true innovator! Anyone can make a topless bathing suit. Anyone can be sensational. He is just a talentless fag coming here to taunt me."

She made hissing noises and pranced around, mocking him with an exaggerated limp wrist. She spit out the window as he drove away.

There was another house on the cul-de-sac, and although I never saw the owner, a hairdresser, except as he came and went in a car, he also received my mother's homophobic wrath.

"I know what you're up to over there with all those young boys coming and going at all hours of the day and night," she'd say as he pulled his convertible into the driveway, a blond, bare-chested male in the passenger seat. "Yell at me one more time, you vicious bitch, and I'll call the police on you!" she'd growl. "I'll report you and your pornographic pursuits!"

I returned from school one day and found her pacing the house like a caged animal. She said she'd gone over there to "have it out with him" and had been "attacked." She turned her arm to show me some faint bruises on the inside of her bicep. She said she was going to sue him for assault and insisted I take photographs of her injuries. She sat on the curb between our homes, her hair pulled back and her arm stretched theatrically alongside her increasingly feral face, as I snapped away. The photos ended up tossed in a drawer, and the threatened lawsuit, like all her pursuits, faded away.

The haunted aspect of my mother's perceptions took a curiously personal and paranoid tone with me. If I asked her who was coming over that night, she would look at me through narrowed eyes and say, "You're a witch. I'm not going to tell you because you know already." She told people I was a reborn Atlantean, a psychic, a tarot card reader. She bought us a Ouija board. She went to see the movie *The Exorcist* and then, regarding me as if I were some sort of a curiosity, refused to tell me what it was about. Eventually, methodically, she explained. The girl in the movie, she said, was about my age, played with a Ouija board just like I did, had a bedroom at the end of a long hallway just like mine, had a window that refused to stay shut just like mine, and a long flight of stairs below that window, exactly like those alongside our house. This girl was possessed by the devil, and because I was a witch, my mother said, she was frightened for me. I became frightened for myself, as well: I stopped playing with the Ouija board and redoubled my completely ineffective efforts to tie the clasps of my window closed.

The Hillside house seemed haunted, too, but with a presence far less benevolent than the spirit who had shared our home on

Fairfax Avenue. I was in my room with a girlfriend one darkening day when I began to get unexplained chills. My friend said I looked strange and asked what was wrong. I said I felt an odd coldness coming from my window, from outside, from that particular side of the house. I felt that something was, simply, inexplicably, very wrong. I went downstairs in the uncharacteristically quiet house to look for my mother and brother and found them clinging to one another in the kitchen, which was directly below my bedroom, looking as if they had just seen a ghost—which, apparently, they had. My mother, in a choked whisper, told me to go shut the side door. Both our dogs, stationed on the threshold, growled low in their throats, frozen on guard. I looked out into the narrow passageway between our house and the one next door and saw, just barely distinct enough to ascertain, a completely still silhouette slightly darker than the surrounding gloom. I called the dogs back and pulled the door shut, and we all clustered in the living room on the opposite side of the house. We lit a fire in the fireplace and huddled together, waiting for the darkness to pass.

But the darkness was around us in other ways. The faux-freedom and pseudo-innocence of the hippie generation was coming to an ignominious end. It was an ending I didn't understand until I read Joan Didion's *The White Album*, where she writes, "Many people I know in Los Angeles believe that the Sixties ended abruptly on August 9, 1969, ended at the exact moment when word of the murders on Cielo Drive traveled like brushfire through the community, and in a sense this is true. The tension broke that day. The paranoia was fulfilled."

I don't remember news of the grizzly and shocking Manson murders she refers to, but I do remember my mother telling us about the trials a year or two later, describing how murderers cut a baby from an actress's stomach and smeared blood over the walls of a home not far from our own. I also remember that the Beatles albums no longer played melodic love songs but now screamed out the dissonance of Helter Skelter. My mother made racist remarks when she spoke about the rise and crash of the Black Panther movement. She sobbed when Richard Nixon was reelected. Patty Hearst appeared in one headline after another, one magazine cover after another, and my mother told us about another young girl lost to so-called revolutionary times. There was a war, a gas crisis, a stock-market crash, a recession.

I didn't think I was psychic or a witch. I didn't think the Ouija board was possessed of real power. But I felt the ombré curtain closing around me in spite of the interminable bright glare of our Southern California days. I didn't discuss my life or my mother's antics with my grandmother, my brother, my teachers. My brother and I sometimes wondered to one another where our mother got money, how she paid whatever bills there were, what the neighbor was referring to when he yelled at her about the red light she left on at night. But we had no answers to these adult quandaries and codes and so tried simply to continue to care for ourselves as best we could.

And we did a good job. To anyone looking on, there would be no real sign for concern in my brother and me, responsible, uncomplaining, excellent-grade-getting children that we were. Once, my mother went to Japan for two weeks with friends. She left us, nine and ten years old, alone at home with a baby-sitter who was instructed to come by only for an hour or two in the evenings, to help with dinner, and then to leave us to put ourselves to sleep and to get ourselves up in the mornings and off to school. After a few nights, the baby-sitter said, "You guys seem to have it all under control. Why don't I just leave my number and you can call me if you need anything?" She went home, and we never called her.

I did write to my father once about the problems facing us at home. He was now living with my stepmother and her son in a rented farmhouse in New Jersey in the midst of a big grassy field surrounded by chestnut trees, an enormous garden hemmed in by the dilapidated stone foundation of what had once been a dairy barn, and a pond across the street. He had called once and found me crying so hard about something my mother had done that I couldn't form actual words to speak to him among the confusion of sobs and hiccups. He'd hung up and said he'd call again, which he didn't do. So I wrote him a letter by way of apologetic explanation. Like my grandmother, I attributed the problems at home, with my mother, and my own hysterics, to drink. I know I was nurturing some very vague hope of rescue, but I didn't know how or what to ask for, so I could only describe some of the conditions of our daily lives.

He finally did call back one day on an unusually quiet weekend afternoon when my mother was out. My body tightened with nerves at the sound of his voice—quiet, cautious, dimmed with the distance of three thousand miles. He said he'd gotten my letter. He asked how I was. And then, in a moment of brilliance that quickly dimmed, he made reference to my coming to him, but instantly added that it was impossible, that I had to keep living with her, it was out of his hands, there was no other way.

This was the second time he'd failed me as a means of escape. Years earlier, when he still lived in L.A., before he moved to New York and then to New Jersey, when I was only four years old and living in the Fairfax house, I'd asked my mother for his phone number. Irritated by the intrusion, she'd snapped at me.

"That's enough, Lolly. I'm sick and tired of you asking me for his phone number. You have a choice to make. I'll give you his number this one last time, but you can never ask me for it again. Or, you have to go live with him."

I took the number. I called my father. I told him that this would be the last time I'd ever be able to call him. I told him what my mother had said. He shocked me by laughing and saying that he'd come over to get me, that I could come stay with him. I couldn't believe it turned out to be this easy.

I'd thought my mother might protest. But she said, "Great," and watched with an amused and patronizing smile as I packed a small bag. She knew him better than I did. I stood in the kitchen with my small satchel waiting for his car to appear in the driveway. She joked with friends sitting at the kitchen table that I was moving out. Wasn't that cute? Wasn't that funny? I stood stoic and resolute. I would show her. I'd have my father all to myself.

For a few days, I did. I played in his garden, at his drafting table. I ate whole-wheat toast and yogurt in his kitchen. I went to sleep in the small, extra bedroom at the back, in the darker side of the house. But when I woke up after two or maybe three days, my bag had been repacked. He told me he was taking me "home." I told him I thought that his house was now home.

"No, silly," he said. "You can't live with me. You have to live with your mom."

My mother laughed at me when I appeared, head down, refusing to meet her eyes, trying not to cry. She asked me how my "vacation" had been. I didn't answer.

"I told you," she said. "You can't trust that bastard."

It was not long after this escapade that my father moved away from California. He told us he was going to New York for work. That it was only for a little while. That he'd send us letters, call us, be back soon. But he didn't come back. He visited us once, unannounced, when I was in fourth grade, surprising Jason and me one afternoon when we were out with classmates on the grammar school playground. He sat with us on a bench while we cried with happiness and confusion, and then he left after only twenty minutes or so. We visited him in New Jersey from time to time. There was little planning. It was haphazard. Once a summer visit bled into a school semester. Other times, months would go by without a phone call or a letter. Years went by without a visit. By the time he moved back to California permanently, I'd already moved East, had been living with him in New Jersey for five years, and was in the middle of college. So by then, his return was really another kind of leaving for me.

Departure

My mother fell in love with a snug bungalow just off Sunset Boulevard, a few blocks from Vine, and a couple of miles from our house on Hillside.

"It's a perfect little dollhouse," she said. "We'll get away from Grandma's prying eyes and all the crazies in this cul-de-sac. I can't take any more of the hostility."

I don't know how she bought it, where the money came from, how or why a bank or her mother stepped in, but when I was around eleven years old, we moved again. The house was smaller and in a worse neighborhood. It had been built for a woman, now going into a nursing home, by her brothers at the time of her marriage. Its front yard faced Hudson Street, its backyard, Wilcox Avenue. There was a porch in front below a generous, central, dormer window that defined the roofline. Inside, there were leaded windows, dark paneling, and elaborate woodwork in compact rooms. There was an elderly person's chairlift in the tight stairwell. There were three bedrooms upstairs, each with an additional, unfinished space under the eaves. My brother took the large, front room. My mother and I each took a smaller bedroom. Mine looked across the driveway and the low concrete wall that separated our property from the parking lot to the tall office building facing Sunset. Hers looked across the side yard where a line of rosebushes against a chain-link fence separated us from the house next door. Another fence, shorter and covered with ivy, marked the line between our tiny backyard and the Wilcox sidewalk. The garage, just big enough to shoehorn in our small car, defined one corner of the backyard. My mother had recently taken her fifteen-year-old Volkswagen to Mexico and had it painted lavender. She then had the house painted to match.

We were much closer to our junior high school, so we could walk instead of taking the bus. But there was no library on the way home, no grandmother's house with meals waiting nearby, no neighbor's house where I was welcome to help feed the baby organic cottage cheese and mashed avocados. And junior high was not the refuge grammar school had been. Instead of tidy young women with smooth hair and modest dresses who frequently singled me out to reward achievement or extra effort, we had mostly overworked, hassled, and harried middle-aged women and men who spent as much time controlling students as teaching subjects. Classes were fuller, materials in shorter supply. Gang members hovered around warehouses outside the school building, their affiliations announced by either red or blue bandannas folded neatly and hanging out the back pockets of their pressed khakis like tongues.

Instead of spending the entire day with a single teacher who became attuned to each student's needs, moods, and skills, we rotated to different classrooms for different subjects throughout the day, and classes in woodworking and sewing were given equal weight to English and social studies. Drugs and fights were commonplace. A teacher trying to break up a playground squabble got punched in the face. A girl tripping on acid had to be restrained from tumbling over a third-story railing outside a classroom. The playground emptied one afternoon as everyone clustered at the far end to watch a fight between girls from the Crips and girls from the Bloods. Only when someone pulled a knife were the police called.

The character of our neighbors changed as well. Most we didn't know, as they lived behind gates and courtyards in ubiquitous stucco apartment complexes. But next door, an elderly woman became an ersatz friend of my mother's. Mrs. Sampson had vodka delivered to the house by the case and drank it in deep swallows from a tall water glass. She frequently stood on her front porch, stark naked except for a falling down pair of men's black socks, two long, white braids hanging over her boiled-potato body and wet-tea-bag breasts, with her gnarled stick legs emerging from either side of her mangy white triangle of pubic hair, calling out to me or some other passersby.

She'd start with, "Hey! Hey, you?" followed by some insistent and incongruous question like, "What are you doing? Where is your wife?" She might exclaim, "My father was Pancho Villa!" Or she'd ask where her drink was, even though the glass in her hand was full. Sometimes she screamed, "What are you looking at?"

Her husband, Ladell, lived with his own cases of vodka in a basement accessed by a low door below a broken flagstone patio of the backyard that abutted ours. She was often heard cursing rhythmically from the threshold of the back door, "Go to hell, Ladell. Ladell, go to hell." She punctuated her demands with a plate or dish thrown ineffectually onto the patio, where it exploded into dozens of sharp-edged shards. Ladell sometimes stood, stooped and sheepish in his subterranean doorway, shrugging his shoulders or lifting his arms, corrugated with sagging flesh, over his head in a pretense of fear. Sometimes my mother and brother chimed in from under the lemon trees in our backyard.

"Ladell, you smell. Go to hell, Ladell," they'd sing out, laughing.

In the mornings, the yelling came from the side door and had a more inviting, almost coquettish tone.

"Yoo-hoo," she'd call, extending each vowel sound for several seconds, her voice dropping from high to low between each note.

My mother would answer in kind, and a prolonged, high-pitched call-and-response would ensue. Then my mother would bring a chair or a stool outdoors and sit in the bed of rosebushes, while Mrs. Sampson, wrapped in a dressing gown, her long hair hanging in loose, snowy cascades over her shoulders, poured vodka through the diamond-shaped openings in the chain-link fence into my mother's coffee cup. They would chatter together among the flowers like two furies, scheming vengeance against the world that had wronged them. Then, without warning, the old woman's mood would change, and her confidential whisperings would become a tirade directed at my mother. She'd chastise her for having too many men around, for being a bad mother, for drinking too much of her vodka. She'd call her a drunk, a "hoor," a disgrace. My mother would laugh at her for a while and then, as the harangue escalated, would stumble back to the house, a bibulous and lopsided smile spread across her face, wiping at the streaks of blood that rose to the surface of her skin from where the thorns had reprimanded her.

My mother had never been a morning drinker. Or a drinker of liquor. She'd never been someone who drank alone. Now she was doing all of these things. I'd been able to make myself believe that although she was a difficult person, perhaps she wasn't a "real" alcoholic; I'd thought she was addicted to attention, to parties, to having people around, and that drinking too much was just an ancillary effect. But this story was wearing thin. A childhood friend once pointed out, "You know, there's no point in getting so upset about your mother being drunk, because after all, she's drunk all the time."

Even more alarming than the drinking was the aura of recklessness and danger that began to permeate my mother's behavior. Because the party no longer came to her, she went looking for it. She ignored our entreaties and cajoling, left the house well after dark, and came home inebriated and trailing men. One morning, I found a couple sprawled on the floor of the living room, blinking against the sunlight; they asked me if their friend was upstairs with my mother or if he'd already left without them. I shook my head, unwilling to look, so they left the house and then so did I. I woke up one night-turning-into-morning to the sounds of slurred words and clumsy footsteps, and I recognized the sound of my mother being hauled upstairs, stumbling and protesting. Then there was a period of silence followed by urgent whispers of strange male voices nearby. I huddled under the blankets in my bed in the dark and musty crawl space. Finally, I heard doors closing downstairs. The next morning, I found my coin bank emptied of my small savings and the two silver dollars my father's father had given me.

The hazard that hung around the men my mother attracted was like a bad smell that began to adhere to me as well. I started to notice their sidelong glances and snickering whispers, as well as my mother's possessive and jealous glares. This routine had begun at the Hillside house. I was standing at the kitchen sink washing dishes one afternoon when she ran out on an errand and left me at home with a young man she had recently met. As soon as her car was out of sight, he came up behind me, slipped his arms around my waist, and whispered something I didn't understand, his voice hot and moist in my ear. I disentangled myself from him, said I had to leave, went out the back door, and kept walking. He was gone when I returned. My mother asked me why I'd left. I was afraid to tell her, unsure what had actually transpired, but eventually the story slipped out. She scrutinized me and nodded. That was it. Until a few weeks later, when I wandered into the living room and found this same man sitting there with her, talking comfortably. His eyes raked my body. My mother's eyes challenged me to question her. Instead, I did what was becoming reflexive: I left the room, the house, the situation.

By the time we got to Hudson Street, my body was filling out, my face was thinning, and my demeanor becoming even graver. When someone asked my age, my answer of "twelve" was often met with a snort of laughter. Then I'd say, "No, really," and the laugh lines would become a furrowed brow, a cautionary stare. But not always.

A dreadlocked musician coming up the driveway one day caught my hands in his as I leaned out a window to tell him my mother was not home, and interrupted me with this sentence: "I would so much like to make love to you." A pale-skinned, hooded-eyed, neon artist in his twenties, who sometimes shared my mother's bed, cornered me in the back pantry on more than one occasion, suggesting in a strained susurrus that I join him sometime for an ice cream, adding that there was no reason to tell my mother, this outing would be our little secret. There was the milk-chocolate colored man with the golden eyes and round face covered with acne scars who played the bass. He told me one night as I sat at the kitchen table, his eyes traveling over the long, gauzy, pale blue nightgown with puffy sleeves I was wearing, that I had no idea how hard it was for men to fight their desires and how dangerous these desires could be. He also told me that I didn't realize how many physical moves and gestures I had picked up from my mother, the way I walked into a room, the way I leaned against a table.

I was horrified and grateful for his counsel. I never wore that nightgown again. I stayed out of rooms where my mother had any kind of male company. I wanted to avoid not just their hungry looks but her vindictive ones as well.

There was one man I had difficulty avoiding. Another musician. He would hold my hand and talk to me while we sat on the sofa or across the table from one another. He would nod sympathetically and encourage me to talk about my mother, my worries. He soothed me with assurances that her behaviors were not my fault, that there was nothing I could do but work hard, stay in school, focus on my own life, grow up as best I could. After weeks of this, he came into my room one night in clingy pajama pants that showed his semi-erection and asked me if he could make love to me. He told me he'd be gentle and that I'd like it. He said other women had told him he was very good at it. I had only a vague idea of what it was he was asking. I shook my head no and turned away from him. He left. But he came back on another night. And then again. I said no, and no again, until some twisted internal logic rose up from inside me and suggested that if I just let him do what he wanted, he'd stop bothering me. So the next time, I didn't say no. I didn't say yes, but I didn't resist. He was gentle. It didn't matter. I didn't respond, it was over in a few moments, and I slipped out from underneath him immediately, filled the bathtub with warm water, and soaked in the dark for hours, wishing I could wash away what had just happened.

My confused logic did have the intended outcome: he never asked me again. Instead, he moved to my mother's bed. She called me into her bedroom one morning on some vague pretext, and he was there, lying beside her. His eyes shot toward me, furtive, uncomfortable. I averted my glance and asked her what she wanted.

"I don't know," she said, her eyes a physical pressure on me. "I forgot."

Some weeks later, they fought over the utility bill he had run up by letting his friends play their electric instruments at the house. He disappeared.

I tried to do the same. I began to carve away at what I ate, moving step by step from two pieces of toast and a yogurt in the morning to half a piece of bread and a spoonful of yogurt; from a burrito and chocolate milk at lunch to half a burrito and half a carton of skim milk. I sat in my room in the dark and did sit-ups and push-ups, working up to a dozen, then twenty-five, then thirty, then fifty. Afraid to go too far away in the dark and with no quiet hills nearby, I ran around the block six, eight, twelve, twenty times. I ran up and down the short, narrow stairwell ten, eighteen, thirty times. I stood on the scale and willed it to move downward. I looked at myself in the mirror and tried to imagine eliminating every glance-inducing curve I had. I looked in the mirror and wanted to see nothing at all.

I got thinner, but this didn't help me hide. The looks continued, and my mother's rage increased.

"This isn't a competition," she'd scream at me, provoked by nothing more than my entering a room where she happened to be. "This isn't a role reversal. I am the mother. You are the daughter. You little bitch. You little fucking cunt."

Like Ladell next door, I'd flinch at her words and then go hide in the dark cave of my room. In contrast, Jason stayed connected to her and found more direct ways to manage her behavior. He hid her jugs of wine or poured out half the vodka and refilled the bottle with water. If she went looking for alcohol she swore she'd just bought or complained about the taste of her drink, he distracted her with a joke or suggested that one of her friends had been drinking more than she'd noticed. When she began to stumble and slur her words, he threw an arm across her shoulder and guided her up the stairs to bed. He told her amusing stories. She laughed with him. But by favoring him, she was also entangling him. I refused her sticky grasp and feared that he was too enamored of the attentions I scorned. She turned on him with less frequency, but when she did, his thin skin took wounds much more easily than the thick carapace I had built up over myself.

I did confront her about her drinking. I was twelve years old and convinced that I was tough enough to try; I had to do something. I knew I was risking her rage, but her continued decline was much more terrifying to me. I had the hope, the belief, that work would save her. If only I could get her to work, I thought, the inherent value and satisfaction of industry would win out over the alcohol. Shaking, my voice quavering, one overcast afternoon when the house was uncharacteristically quiet, I asked if I could talk to her. She sat with me at the kitchen table below the meat hook she'd painted purple and used to hang pots, pans, and other cooking implements. I told her I was worried about her drinking. I told her that I wasn't judging her, but I was concerned; I wanted to see her painting again or designing clothes again, and I thought her drinking was getting in the way of that much more important work. She kept her eyes down and nodded thoughtfully. She fussed with her hands.

Then she stood and mastering the wobble in her voice said, "Well, thank you. I understand what you've said, and I'll give it some thought. I appreciate your concern."

She left the room. I sat in amazement that she had listened and allowed myself the small luxury of wondering what life might be like if she stopped drinking. But this short calm only presaged a storm the likes of which I had not seen before. Moments later, she was back in the room.

"You fucking cunt," she hissed at me. "Who the fuck do you think you are, telling me what to do, you ungrateful little know-nothing bitch?"

I got up and walked out of the room. She followed me.

"After all I've done for you! I've given you everything. How dare you question me? How dare you! You stinking brat!"

I wandered the house, her epithets at my back, until with nowhere else to go I went out the front door. Her voice followed me into the yard.

"Don't come back, you little shit. I don't care if I ever see you again."

Jason found me in the yard, crying.

"She hates me," I said.

"She's never going to change," he said.

"You guys get along. She adores you. You like the same things."

"We're both Geminis," he said. We were quiet. Then he said, "Maybe you should go live with Dad."

175

He'd written to us not too long ago, saying that he had bought a farmhouse. It was old, it needed a lot of work, but he was going to fix it up. It had barns with plenty of room for goats, horses, chickens. It was on five acres and had two fenced pastures and a stream at the bottom of the hill. It had been a few years since we'd seen him.

"Maybe you could get a horse," Jason said. "It would be better for you. You don't like L.A. anyway."

I don't recall how it happened. Somehow, a call must have been made, or a letter was written, and a ticket was arranged. There was no plan for a permanent move. My father and I would both have been too afraid to suggest that, he for fear of the responsibility, me for fear of having my hopes dashed. My mother had her own fears.

"If you leave here, don't bother coming back," she said, over and over again. "I don't ever want to see you again."

Then she'd start to twist her hands and sob.

"Don't leave me," she'd moan. "You can't leave me. You're abandoning me. Everyone always abandons me."

Other times she'd try this: "Go ahead, go to that bastard, your father," she'd say. "You'll see. Just you wait. You'll find out what a liar he is. He's just seducing you with horses, the prick. He just wants you there so you can work on his farm."

Then she'd start crying again.

"You're going to wreck your body. You're going to get fat and get ugly muscles in your legs riding horses. You're going to ruin your hands with all that manual labor. He's going to make you ugly," she'd warn.

I left nine days after my thirteenth birthday, carrying a small suitcase filled with my few belongings—some clothes, a couple of books, a stuffed animal my father had gotten for me years earlier. I got off the plane in New Jersey noticeably underweight, with over-plucked eyebrows and thin, dirty blond hair, wearing a slinky, black, low-cut, wrap-around dress with a large, sequin rose at the waistband, chunky, platform, lace-up heels, and a floppy hat. I had wanted to dress up to see my dad. This was how I thought it was done.

My stepmother said I looked like I was thirteen going on thirty.

She was right.

And so was my mother. I did put on weight. I did carry buckets, heave hay bales, dig in the garden, shovel horseshit, milk goats, get calluses on my hands, dirt under my fingernails, and big muscles in my legs. I found out that my father did have his own, rather elusive way with the truth. I also never lived with her again.

$\mathcal{T}$eenager

Although living with my father, stepmother, and stepbrother was more stable and tenable than what I'd left in California, it did present its own strange brew of contradictions, disconnects, and confusions that made us an awkward bunch on even the best of days.

My father had purchased five acres about an hour west of New York City on a main street in a small town that was somewhat country but quickly becoming suburban, with real farms morphing into gentleman farms and, in some cases, McMansion developments. The denizens were almost exclusively old money-wielding, country club–attending, social register–consulting, Republican-voting, Wall Street–employed, Labrador retriever and thoroughbred horse–owning, tassel-loafered families.

My father had longish hair worn in a frizz around his head, favored open-necked, patterned shirts and wide-wale corduroys. He worked from his own small office in midtown, designing museum exhibitions and commercial interiors, and struggled to keep enough work coming in consistently enough to stay ahead of the bills that often arrived with angry, red, impending shut-off notice lines across the top of the envelope.

My stepmother dyed her hair carrot red, adorned her fingers with a collection of layered rings, had a gay hairdresser for a best friend, and pursued various food-related activities from making goose liver *pâté* to writing about herbs. My stepbrother, a year younger than I, was sweet and self-contained, interested in watching baseball and running track, and attended a private school with an alternative curriculum, courtesy of some wealthy relatives. I took to shoveling manure to support my horse habit and was bused to the public school a few towns away.

Everyone drove Volvos, BMWs, or SUVs the size of small apartments; we had an old Datsun. Many homes around us included mudrooms cluttered with hunting jackets, field boots, saddlery, horse-show ribbons, and dog bowls. Formal dining rooms were adorned with china, silver, and crystal passed down from previous generations, pools with lounge chairs where a maid might bring out chicken-salad sandwiches and fizzy drinks made with grape juice and ginger ale. Grooms kept horses and horse barns neat and tidy, and white-fenced pastures included riding rings, complete with jumps and instructors who arrived once a week to try to instill discipline in the household's teenage girls before they traded their interest in horses for boys. I mucked stalls and rode the horses no one else would. My classmates went to the country club, attended cotillions, and had charge accounts at the saddle shop; we went to SoHo to visit artist friends who lived in warehouse lofts and worked in neon. I had never heard of L.L. Bean, Lily Pulitzer, Izod, paddle tennis, deck shoes, or debutante balls. I came from a school with gangs defined by race; at my new school, they had cliques defined by breast size and boyfriends.

Our home was valued at zero when my father purchased the property, which was the only reason he could afford to buy it. He had drawn up elaborate plans that included brick patios, cherry cabinets and bookshelves, period-appropriate herb gardens, a fruit orchard with an espaliered pear tree, an open kitchen, designer fabrics on the furniture, Colonial paint colors, molding and trim details, dormered windows, and more, more, more. He managed to take most of the house apart in preparation for these restorations but kept running out of money before he could put it back together again. Raw, galvanized electric boxes hung from the ceiling, floors were made of plywood or linoleum left over from decades before, a small potbellied stove supplied the only heat for the dining and kitchen areas, and our bedroom walls were adorned with just the silvery backside of fiberglass insulation as they awaited Sheetrock.

In New Jersey, I tried, from time to time, to be a teenager. I went to school and was promoted to the honors program. I made some friends and went to some parties. I took long walks through real woods and fields instead of scrub hillsides. My dad and I cleaned up the barn, built stalls and a tack room; I leased a sturdy buckskin quarter horse mare, rented stalls to make enough money to support the both of us, and showed her in events alongside the rich girls' sleek, dark thoroughbreds. I worked in the gardens, learned to recognize herbs by rubbing them between my fingers and inhaling the smells, pruned roses so the new growth would extend outward. I held up Sheetrock while my dad hammered in nails, milked the goats my father acquired, went sledding in the wintertime, helped my stepmother make pasta and pork chops for dinner, and most nights ate at a table with all four of us seated together, talking about our day. Jason joined us for almost a year of high school, trying to escape as I had, but he and my father fought, their personalities always at odds with one another. He didn't like the East Coast and longed for California.

The only significant disruption to this ungainly balance we'd achieved came on those occasional nights, often months and months apart, when the dark red phone in the kitchen would ring at an odd hour, signaling a call from someone in California unconcerned about the time difference. Although I don't recall ever discussing my former living situation with my father or stepmother, and I don't recall their ever asking about it either, they both knew my mother and her ways. So we all ducked our eyes in concern and flinched at the sound of the ringer as we waited for me to muster up enough fortitude to pick up the receiver.

"Lolly Dolly?" my mother would say at the sound of my mumbled hello, her voice pushed into strange and dramatic peaks and valleys.

"Yes, Mom. I'm here."

"Well, you didn't sound like it!" she'd snort. "Listen, Lolly, so much has gone on since you left. I can't even begin to tell you everything you've been missing."

"Really," I'd breathe into the phone. "Well, why don't you tell me some of what's going on out there."

I was listening for the echo of alcohol in her voice. Sometimes I found it, but there seemed to be less and less difference between the drunk and sober versions of my mother.

"Well, we had such a gathering last weekend," she'd rush on. "It was a *happening*! There were musicians and artists making music and art in the backyard. We're taking all the broken pieces of my precious artifacts and creating a beautiful mosaic pond. It's already bringing in the wildlife, and honey, I'm talking about human wildlife, as well as the other kind. I'm making an oasis in the middle of this Hollywood Hell. Your darling brother came and entertained us with tales from Hollywood High. Your friend Tina stopped by with some very cute young man. Oh, she's as adorable as ever. She hasn't changed a bit since she was in first grade. My favorite duck, Miss Covi, is making a nest in the ivy. The neighbors are threatening to have all the ducks taken away. They say I'm harboring wildlife. I tell them I don't harbor it, I simply attract it!"

"Sounds like fun, Mom," I'd reply. But it didn't. It sounded like everything I'd left, everything I never wanted to be a part of again. Her puns and witticisms made me flinch.

"You're missing it all," she'd say, her voice false and light. "Everybody asks about you. I tell them you've flown the coop. They ask when I'm expecting your return. I tell them that you don't share your plans with me. Your own mother."

I would slide to the floor of the pantry, my body curled into a question mark against the wall. I had no plans to share with her. I had no thought of my future beyond next weekend's party, next month's horse show. I hadn't really made the decision to move to New Jersey; I'd only made the decision to leave Los Angeles. I'd never really made the decision to stay in New Jersey either; I just never made the decision to return to Los Angeles. The only thing I felt I actively wanted was to spend my time in the relative peace and quiet of the barn, around animals whose needs were simple and straightforward, who received my attentions with neutrality, who didn't talk to me at all.

I might manage to tell her this much: "I'm happy here, Mom."
"Oh, really," she'd say, her voice larded with sarcastic disbelief.
"Yes," I'd say quietly. "I feel like this is where I'm supposed to be now. I think this is the right place for me. They just put me into an honors program at high school. I'm making some new friends. I'm doing well with my horse and my horse-boarding business. I have a new instructor, and I won a ribbon at the event last weekend and...."

"Lolly, that is just all so, so, so bore-ing."

I'd close my eyes and rub my back teeth against one another, a headache starting to pulse in time to the grinding of my molars and my memories.

"Lolly, you are just wasting yourself!" she'd blurt out. "I'm telling you, that bastard is just using you as a farmhand. I can tell you're getting fat. Full of masculine muscles with calluses on your hands and horseshit on your clothes."

I would wait for her to wear herself out.

"Now you listen to me. I gave you gifts, and you should be using them. You're near New York now. You go get someone to take pictures of you and take them to the modeling agencies. In a day, you could make more than you do in a month. You are just ruining yourself slaving in that barn. In New Jersey of all places! New Jersey is nothing but a pit, a shit-hole for losers!"

I wanted to say, no, no, no, that's all for you, not for me. I'm not tall enough or pretty enough or skinny enough. Even if I were, I don't want to be a model; I don't want to have my picture taken. I don't care about any of that. I don't want to finish what you started. I don't want to succeed where you failed. You'd only hate me more than you already do, you'd only resent me more.

But I said nothing.

"Lolly, are you listening to me? I had great photographers take pictures of you. They said you were the most photogenic girl they'd ever seen. Of course you are. You are my daughter. Come back here right now and stop all that foolishness."

Her voice would disintegrate into a growl.

"You are making me so mad!"

My voice would come out in a croak. "Mom, this is where I need to be. It's where I want to be."

"You've abandoned me, Lolly. I will never forgive you for it. Go ahead, go ahead and ruin yourself. I don't care anymore. I can't keep caring. I've had enough. That's it. I'm never calling you again."

The line would go dead. I would slump, a plant desiccated by the harsh wind of my mother's words. Even at this distance, she stayed with me. I got headaches that felt as if half my face were sliding off my skull. I was tired enough of the time that a teacher pulled me aside to discuss my sleeping habits. I had a watchfulness about me, scanning the skies for impending clouds even on a clear day. I fretted, I worried, and then I went out to the barn and tried to ride away from the dark cloud that only I could see. I took long walks through the still, open fields and tried to wear away the cicatrix of my past with her. Sometimes, I lay in a dark room with a cold, damp cloth across my forehead. Sometimes I cried myself to sleep.

Occasionally, I spoke to Jason. I hated to ask, because he was still there, the only one hanging on, trying to have a life of his own and to hold the shreds of hers together as well. He gave abbreviated updates. A description of a party at the house. A mention of the ducks that had congregated in the backyard. Some passing reference to a fight or a blow-up that sent him to Grandma's house for some time. He told the stories with a studied flippancy that I feared—that I knew—hid deeper agonies and worries.

He usually ended the conversation with this observation: "She's just being Mom, Laurel."

Shorthand captured everything she was, and everything we were unable to do about it.

* * *

I returned to California a few years after leaving. This visit was probably at the suggestion of my grandmother, as I stayed with her. I was fretful and ambivalent about seeing my mother but felt duty-bound to try to visit her at the house on Hudson. She was elusive.

"I don't know, Lolly. I just don't know when I'll be here. I have important appointments to keep. There's so much going on. You'll just have to stop by."

I didn't just want to stop by. For the first time in my life, I wanted something specific and concrete from her, and I wanted it badly enough to ask, and to ask again and again; I wanted her to paint me. Her obsession was with getting me to model; mine was with getting her to work. I held onto the sliver of an idea that if she could be induced to paint, she'd start to recover. That if we could work together to get her painting again, some lost part of her would be restored. I was also alarmed at her decline. I was afraid of everything that was being destroyed. I wanted some memento of my own, something I could hold onto.

"I don't have anything you've ever done. I don't have a single painting of yours," I said. "I'd really like to have a painting of yours. I'd like you to paint me," I said, trying to hide the desperation beneath my desire.

185

"I don't know," she said, hesitating. "I don't know where my paints are. I'm not sure I have any paper. I'll have to look...."

"We'll find them, Mom. We can even go get new stuff. I just want to have something of yours. Something that you've done."

I felt panicked. Some part of me recognized that time was running out for her. For us. That if I were to see any evidence of her artistic productivity, if I were to have any legacy besides the mania contained in her phone calls and letters, the pain of my own memories, I needed to get it on this trip.

Finally, we picked a time to get together. My grandmother dropped me off at Hudson Street, her mouth creased into a tight line of worry. I waved her off, went up the front steps of the porch, past the broken wicker chairs and creaking porch swing. The front room was dark. I called to my mother. No answer. I walked slowly through the house. I finally found her in the back room, off the kitchen. She was shuffling in a drawer. She looked up startled, like a hungry animal surprised while rummaging through garbage.

"Oh, Lolly. You frightened me."

Her eyes jumped and popped with some erratic, internal fire stoked only by sodden and decaying logs. She scuttled out the far door into a small, pink-tiled bathroom. I followed her slowly, at a careful distance.

"Mom? Mom? Is everything OK?"

I peered around the open door. She was looking at her face in the mirror, angry, dissatisfied. Then she looked at me and ran away again. The hem of the long, red-and-white striped caftan she was wearing flashed through the other door. I crossed the bathroom and found her in the far corner of the small, first floor bedroom. There was a large mattress littered with a few rumpled blankets and some makeup-stained pillows. There were two or three large moving boxes up against a wall, still unpacked from when we came to this house years earlier. There was a dressing table cluttered with lipstick and mascara tubes, a silk scarf, some stray mail, a dirty coffee mug, a glass half-filled with water. She was staring out the window into the side yard.

"I moved down here," she said. "Too many crazies upstairs." Her voice had gone soft.

I stayed very still, waiting for her next move.

"I can make my escapes more easily from here," she said, matter-of-factly. "If intruders come in the back, I slip out the front. If they come in the front, I go out the back."

"It's a nicer room, in any case," I said. "Bigger windows. Better light. You have your own bathroom."

"I can see the roses," she said, her eyes looking away, out the window.

Her eyes were puffy with swollen pouches underneath. Her skin was blotchy, her nose reddened. Her bangs were cut at an awkward angle, her hair ragged at the ends. She had not put on any makeup.

"Mom," I said, softening my voice as much as possible. "Mom, do you think we could do that painting? I really would so love to have something by you to have with me forever."

She covered her face with her hands and started to weep.

"Oh, Lolly," she sobbed. She held out her hands. "Look, look at these! They're ruined."

Her nails were chipped, her fingers swollen, and the back of her hands creased. She turned her palms up.

"Just look! How can I paint with these?"

There were a few calluses, some slender cuts that could have been made by opening an envelope, slipping with a paring knife, or trimming rosebushes. She pulled a crumpled tissue from the pocket of her dress and blew her nose loudly.

187

"I just need to give myself a manicure," she said, pointing her chin in the air, steadying her voice. "I can't do anything until I give myself a manicure."

"OK," I said. "I'll help you."

Her face crumpled in on itself again.

"But I can't find any polish. I can't find my nail file. That's what I was looking for when you came in. All my polish is dried up or gone."

I stepped up to her. I took her trembling hands in my own.

"Mom, there's nothing wrong with your hands." I spoke carefully. "See, Mom. This is why I want you to paint again. This is why you need to get back to what you're supposed to be doing. If you could paint again and do the work you love, your hands...they'd be beautiful again. They'd be doing what they were intended to do."

She organized her mouth and jaw back into their usual planes. She blinked hard a few times. She pulled her hands away from mine, dabbed at her eyes.

"All right, Lolly." Her tone was officious. "All right. I just have to find some paper. Some paints."

She brushed past me. I followed her through the house. She went into the kitchen, opening and slamming drawers, scrounging among bits of broken plates, unmatched cutlery, wine corks, and candle ends. She found a black pen here, a couple of old paintbrushes there. She pulled a jelly jar from a cabinet and filled it with water. She rushed into the dining room and found a pad of paper under a pile of notebooks in the china cabinet. She flew past me again, into the living room, where she found a palette covered with dried clumps and washes of watercolors among some bits of lace, a feather boa with most of the feathers gone, a swatch of tie-dyed, crushed velvet. In another drawer, among some spools of thread and ribbons, she found a small box with about a dozen tiny tubes of paint.

"These were yours!" she said, holding them aloft, as if she'd discovered buried treasure. "Do you remember? We bought these in Chinatown." Her voice softened. "When you were just a little girl. When you were my Lolly Darling. Before you went away."

"Yes, Mom, I remember," I said. I tried to make my voice appropriately sad but not defeated. "I think it's perfect that you'll paint me with paints from my childhood. Where would you like me to sit?"

She waved me toward the bay window where the sun was streaming in. She pushed at a few large pillows, orange with white Chinese characters, to create a companionable arrangement around me. She found a chair and collected her paints and implements on a small table with a marble top. She sat with the pad propped up in her lap and swirled her brushes in the jar of water. She opened and squeezed one of the tubes.

"Ack. These paints are so dry." She tried another tube. "Oh shit," she said, and her eyes filled with tears again. "I don't know, Lolly. I don't know if this is going to work."

I watched her fight within herself, her fears and her talents clashing. I was afraid that instead of showing her what she could regain, I was only revealing all that she had lost.

"There," she said, suddenly composed as a hardened plug popped out, followed by a snake of pigment.

I settled back against the pillows. Her little brown dog, the one Jason had found as a puppy being given away outside a grocery store, now grizzled and with only one eye, jumped up and nestled under my arm against my thigh. My mother fanned out her pens and pencils. She scrubbed the tips of various pens against a corner of the tablet, looking for one that still had ink flowing. She avoided looking at me.

But then, finally, she did. Her eyes became brighter, more focused. She wasn't seeing me; she saw a subject to be painted. She sat up taller in her chair, propped the pad upright, poised a pen above the paper, and then, like a gymnast beginning a routine, plunged full speed into the painting. Her eyes flicked back and forth from me to the page. Her hands moved in quick strokes. Her pen scratched across the textured surface. Her brush dabbed into the soft, sad clumps of paint. Her head tilted back and forth, a metronome keeping time between her subject and her work. I froze in place, terrified to interrupt the flow of her energy, her industry.

"God, Lolly," she said. "Your thighs are so big. All that horse-back riding and shit shoveling. I have to keep moving my line farther and farther out. I'm going to run out of paper."

I dropped my eyes and let my fingers caress the dog, swallowing hard against the insult. I focused my thoughts on what I wanted, on what I hoped I was getting from her. When I finally looked up again, my mother's movements had slowed and her expression had begun to close in on itself like an animal in retreat. Her eyebrows tightened. Her jaw twitched a few times. She fumbled her stroke. She plucked a different brush from the jar of graying water. I saw her shiver.

"Are you cold?" she asked me.

"No, Mom, I'm fine." The room was warm.

"I'm always so cold. I can't ever seem to get warmed up," she said.

Her hands started to shake, her control over the brush fading.

"All right. That's enough," she said, her arm making a few final staccato moves across the page.

She stood, turned her back to me, and propped the pad of paper against the chair. I couldn't see what she'd done. I was terribly afraid she'd made me ugly. Then she stepped aside, and a young woman, not a girl of fifteen, looked out at me from the page. Her doe eyes glanced sidelong toward the left of the canvas. Her mouth was set but not rigid. Her medium brown hair fanned out over her shoulders, with the sides swept back from her face. She wore brown pants and had a sensuous curve to her hip and thigh, a nipped-in waist, the suggestion of full breasts. Her hands were unfinished, a few strokes depicting just the curve of fingers. A fruit-laden orange-tree bough had been painted into the window, although none existed in the yard. There were some rough spots where the paints seemed not willing to cooperate, where the color was too thin, too scuffed, or dry. But the composition was elegant, the brown hair, pants, and dog forming a triangle grounded by the bright orange fruit and pillows, and around which spots of yellow, green, and pink created a lively backdrop.

The woman on the page should have been pretty. But her expression, watchful and alert as if dangers were lurking, kept her potential beauty at bay. I was relieved. It looked like me. It was something I wanted to keep. It showed the best of my mother's talents. She'd rallied just enough of her reserves to make this thing for me, to give me evidence of the woman she'd once been.

"Thank you, Mom."

I looked at her, looking at the picture. Her eyes were jittery. Her mouth twitched.

"Ugh. I can't…if only I'd been able to find my paints. Well… there, Lolly. There you are. Take it. Take it away."

I brought the painting back to New Jersey and had it framed. It's hung somewhere in every home I've had since. When people visiting see it, they usually ask who it's of. They are surprised when I tell them. They pause, wonder, say things like "Hunh. I didn't guess. I was going to ask if you had a sister. It doesn't really look like you."

But it does. It looks like the girl I was when I was around my mother. It's a person no one but me recognizes.

A Final Conversation

I began college early, after my junior year of high school, at age sixteen. I was bored and distracted academically, and when I found a college that accepted high school students, I leaped at the chance to skip my senior year and jump straight into college. A year later, I transferred to New York University, and a year or so after that, my father and stepmother moved back to California. I stayed in the still barely improved farmhouse, pruning the roses, mowing the lawn, watching the dog and cat, working a few days a week, commuting to NYU where I jammed my classes into two long days, and visiting my boyfriend of three years at his college in upstate New York on weekends when I could.

Jim was a gentleman, the first person who formally asked me out to dinner for our first date, who held doors open for me, bought me flowers, wrote me long letters, and even got into his car late at night and drove the two-and-a-half hours to my house to be with me if he found I'd had a bad day. I'd told him some stories about my mother. Mostly as a way of telling him about myself: I looked at my past primarily as a means to explain why I didn't like to get drunk like other kids our age and why, even more, I hated to be around people who were drunk. I thought my childhood explained my sensitivity and why I was given to unexplained sadnesses. My early years also seemed to contain within them the reason for speaking little about them. I had been far enough away for long enough to begin to think that perhaps the past was just that—past. I had been told so many times by the people who had received an abbreviated description of my mother's life—and by implication, my life with her—that my experiences had shaped me into the mature, secure person I was, that I was beginning to believe it. I was still too young to realize that sensitivity didn't require an explanation and that I could value my strength without discounting the pain of the experiences that had earned it.

Jim and I were planning a trip to California to visit my father to attend the opening of the first exhibit of the Los Angeles Museum of Modern Art. The show was being held in a former police garage while the so-called permanent museum was still under construction; my father had designed the exhibition of American painting and sculptures from 1940–1980. I didn't know if I would see my mother while we were on the West Coast. I didn't know if I could even track her down. For the past several years, I'd only gotten fractured bits of information. She might or might not be living in the house on Hudson Street. She'd sold it. But she'd kept living there. For a while anyway. Then she'd been kicked out.

Or maybe she'd just left. She'd somehow bought an empty lot in Ventura. She would go up there and camp out. But it was in the middle of a suburban neighborhood so people were complaining. She made campfires. This was a serious offense in wildfire-prone Southern California. She'd been arrested for vagrancy.

There were few things to be gleaned from my occasional communications with her. She had sent me a letter addressed to "Dollie Lollie," in which she wrote that Owen "…had boxes of our lives dumped in the backyard. He ordered my life-time collection of museum pieces moved out of my home while advertising an estate sale in the newspapers without informing ME! the maternal keeper of priceless personal possessions…. My enemies are attempting to possess my work and possessions and remove my sanity. It is a brutal nightmare. But the angels guarding me with protective wings…keep me one jump ahead of the conspiracy."

Included in the envelope was a round, flower-shaped piece of stationery on which she'd written in a spiral that she was delayed sending the letter because "a savage slithered around the corner of my kitchen with a knife poised in hand and threatened to hurt me. I lectured the beast about right and wrong and he left apologizing." She ended the letter with "I can only send what I have to send to you, darling—which is Infinite love from Anne D'arc."

Her protestations of love always caused me to cringe in discomfort at what I felt were the false heart of her expressions and guilt at my own lack of reciprocal emotion. But I tried to discern reality from her embellishments. I could see Owen setting up a garage sale, I just couldn't see why. Of course, she would have enemies, but I knew her own impossible behavior infuriated people and turned them against her. I could clearly imagine a would-be attacker thwarted by the force of her grandiose self-absorption, the formidable sight of her in an indignant rage at his temerity. The scene would have been almost comical if it weren't so frightening.

After the house on Hudson Street burned, she sent me an envelope stuffed with several blackened and water-damaged photos of me as a child, something I received as a rebuke for having been there in likeness only instead of in person. In another letter, she exhorted me, "So don't believe the vile insidious lies which are circulating about your mother. They are but rationalizations of the cruel plans they have to cheat me of all I honestly worked for. My relatives are conspiring to institutionalize me to shut up the truth and light I shed on their sordid little existence." She went on to tell me that she'd been "savagely beaten by the dangerous terrorist occupying my house…," that she'd been "thrust out in the rain and cold on winter's nights repeatedly," that she'd "reached the bottom." But she finished her letter by saying, "I shall emerge triumphant in fresh sparkling rebirth this new year with a new name! Aurora Rises!"

I could only shake my head and feel my stomach turn in astonishment at the infallibility and single-mindedness of her mania. And then, as she had done throughout my childhood, she exhorted me once again to pursue modeling. "As you know, beautiful young girls are the rage currently. It is time you cashed in as a cover girl. Just put on makeup and chic outfits and show the big shots what you can do…."

I can do nothing, I thought. I'm not pretty enough or dramatic enough, and I don't like makeup and chic outfits and vamping for the camera enough. And what did modeling do for you, I asked her silently in my head, other than make you vain and give you a corrupting sense of entitlement?

I trembled as I read these letters, guilt and duty running circles in my gut, their nails scratching the walls of my stomach. She wanted something from me I wouldn't, couldn't, ever give her: total, self-destroying loyalty and idolatry. I had escaped early; my brother had stayed entangled, enjoying the adoration she denied me when we were both children but suffering more and longer later on from her cruel words. They pelted us both like stones but also bounced off me more readily, used as I was to turning a hard shoulder toward them. I simultaneously stuffed and held farther at bay my emotions about her, a trick distance made possible.

Now, facing a trip to California, my beloved, gentle, suburban teenage boyfriend by my side, my emotions felt like hot grease in a frying pan. When I asked my father and brother what I should do, they shrugged and suggested I do whatever I wanted but not to go out of my way.

"You know what she's like. You know how she is," they'd say.

Which I was afraid I didn't, anymore. This made me want to and not want to see her in equal measure.

For most of the days I was in California, I avoided making any decisions or any moves about her. We went to the museum opening, an important event for Los Angeles that signaled its escape from a supposedly empty cultural frontier into a buzzing center for art. As I wandered the open warehouse space, I was surprised at how many little white tags next to the artwork held names I recognized. Altoon, Bengston, Kauffman, Oldenburg, Ruscha—all my mother's former friends. I wondered if any of these artists remembered her, ever thought of her, wondered what ever happened to Annie Ford. She seemed a shadowy presence at the gallery, a mangy stray scratching listlessly at the back door, not allowed in.

I continued agonizing and stalling about what to do. Then the phone rang. She said she'd heard I was in town. She asked me to drive to Ventura to see where she was "living." I told her I didn't know. There wasn't much time. I had no car. It was long drive. What I thought but didn't say was that I was scared to see her, scared of the effect seeing her would have on me. And I wondered what I owed her, as a daughter yes, but a daughter she'd treated like shit her whole life. I told her I'd see what I could do. I asked her to call back in a day or two.

"Why," my father asked when I hung up the phone, "would you want to put yourself through that?"

Because she's my mother, I said to myself, recognizing finally the raw power of the straightforward fact of heredity. But self-preservation pushed me equally hard to avoid her. Or perhaps it was cowardice. I knew I could stand seeing her, but I also knew the toll it would take on me: I'd become a ruin of tumbled and broken bits of emotion that it could take weeks to rebuild.

Instead, she found me. It was one of the last days of our trip. Jim and I had stopped by my grandmother's house to say good-bye. We walked in the back door and called hello as we moved into the house. My grandmother rushed from the kitchen, her face drawn, her eyes agitated, her hands up in a protective, cautionary stance.

"What's wrong?"

"She's here," Grandma whispered, gesturing frantically toward the kitchen.

"How is she?"

My grandmother could only shake her head a few times in answer. I asked Jim to wait in the den. I had no idea what her condition might be; I needed to see her first. I walked tentatively through the kitchen. I tried to sound light, cheerful, but my voice was a thin sound in my tightened throat.

"Mom? Mom, are you here?"

I found her in the corner of the laundry room, pacing, her eyes blazing with a dark light. She was wearing a cheap sundress of some thin material, her ample breasts swinging freely, her bloated stomach pushing against the fabric, her hands and bare feet rimmed with dirt, her nails split, her hair long and unkempt. Her expression was febrile. I lowered my voice and spoke slowly, as if she were a frightened, stray dog.

"Hi, Mom. I'm glad to see you."

"Is he here? Is your boyfriend here?"

"Yes, Mom. He's here." I paused. "He'd like to meet you."

This was true, even though there was nothing in his experience, in my few tales, that could prepare him for this.

Then she startled me with an act so piteous, so unlike her, so full of awareness of her own degradation, that I almost burst into tears. She looked down at herself, her eyes full of anguish, then at me, pride struggling with shame, and, frantically shaking her hands at everything she'd become, wailed, "I can't! I can't meet him like this!"

She swept past me, running away. I spun and followed her through the kitchen, the dining room, the den.

Jim stuck out his hand as she passed, innocently, unfailingly, absurdly polite. "Pleased to meet you," he said.

She touched his hand without pausing, nodded, and then skittered out the back door. I jogged past the worried eyes of my grandmother and the confusion of my boyfriend and trotted along the driveway behind her.

"Please, Mom. Please, come back. C'mon, Mom. Just come back inside. We'll talk a little. Mom. Mom."

"I can't, Lolly," she said over her shoulder, swiping at tears, her voice a groan.

And then she spit her chewed-up agony onto someone else.

"I can't stay in that house with her, that horrible bitch, that cunt, that witch, for one more minute."

The words intended for my grandmother hit and bounced off me, leaving small, sore divots behind. I kept following her anyway, as she went out the door, down the drive, through the gate, to the sidewalk where she'd parked her car, a yellow convertible Volkswagen Bug that my grandmother had bought her a few years earlier. I wondered how I could have missed the car-as-warning when I came in, but I thought only of her turquoise-then-lavender Beetle. She flung open the passenger side door, and I thought she would shove over and drive away, but instead, she dropped to the seat and stared at her toes curled against the curb. I checked my own forward motion, took a breath, and sat down next to her dirty feet, my head bent in humble supplication to the queen on her debased throne.

She launched into a tirade filled with disjointed tales of bumming cigarette butts, sleeping on the beach, wearing shoddy clothes, having no shoes, being put in jail on vagrancy charges. But for every degradation, she also had a counter charm. She said she lived freely and would never be confined again. She told me she organized and inspired the girls in jail to stand up for themselves, painted their portraits, made the judge laugh, had the entire court in stitches with her puns and witticisms. She said she looked fabulous and fashionable in her prison jumpsuit, its rich blue shade bringing out the blue/gray/green of her eyes. She described the plans she'd drawn up for the restoration of her home, complete with a roof made of glass so she could always see the stars. Angels and flower children would come down from the hills, up from the beach, out of the jails, and build Queen Anne her castle, she knew it, she said, she deserved it, she'd be vindicated.

I said nothing, only nodding and murmuring sounds of assent. I thought of my grandmother back in the house, wringing her hands, peering out the front window. I thought of Jim and knew that he would be worrying for me. I could think of nothing to do other than sit, listen, and let her run out of words. Her hysteria wound down. The hunted look left her eyes. She was less frightened and frightening. She began to look lost, out of place, vaguely confused, like someone who woke up in a place different from where she went to sleep.

She has her fantasies to sustain her, I thought. I have none. Fantasies were something I had refused even as a child, never believing in things like the tooth fairy or Santa Claus. It was clear to me that my mother would never recover from her own life. I felt like a dirty towel with all the water wrung out.

Tentatively, she asked if I was having a good time on my "vacation." She said the word with distaste.

I said I was.

She asked when I was leaving.

Soon.

"So, I won't see you again?"

I shook my head. Then I thanked her for coming, for driving such a long way to see me. It was more than I had done for her. We parted without touching. I got up and walked away, back into the house, back to my agitated grandmother, my concerned boyfriend, my life.

I never saw my mother again.

* * *

Less than a year later, I was once again making plans to go to California, this time for Thanksgiving with my father. Again,

I didn't know what to do about my mother, whether to search her out, whether to tell her I was going to be there. Every time I thought of her, I got unbearably, enervatingly sad.

Then I wrote her a letter, an outward act of an interior realization: I had always held myself in abeyance around her. Assured of her rejection and ridicule, I kept myself hidden and never shared the full force of my interests, accomplishments, self. I decided that because I had nothing to lose, I would present myself to her as fully as I could. I would then know, I thought, that I had at least done that much. The decision to write had come to me in that flash of clarity that occurs when an action has been silently, subconsciously, building momentum inside.

I told her that I was in a special honors program at college, editor of our college literary magazine, doing volunteer work helping handicapped people ride horses, working part-time at a division of the *New York Times*, paying my way through college, still dating Jim, now four years after we'd met. I wrote that although I realized she didn't approve of the choices I'd made, I did. I told her I was happy leading this life so different from the one she would have chosen for me and wished she could be the same. I sent the letter off and expected nothing from her, contenting myself with the simple act of self-expression. Then a couple of weeks later, while sitting in the kitchen of the old farmhouse with Jim and another friend, the phone rang. We had been joking about something, so laughter was still in my voice when I picked up the phone and said hello.

"Lolly?"

Her voice was unmistakable but also somehow different. Calm, without its usual ragged edge, its tilting toward chaos.

"Hi, Mom."

At these words, my friends stopped talking and turned toward me, their eyes filled with alarm. I shrugged and gave them a tentative, quizzical smile. They had made me happy, secure, loved. My life had made me feel that way, too. Her voice, finally, didn't scare me. I felt almost ready, willing to talk to her.

"I can't talk long," she said. "I'm at George's. You know, my neighbor from across the street on Hudson. He's always loved me, been loyal to me."

I registered her rebuke. I had done and been neither of those things.

"Well, as you know," she continued, "I have no utilities, no phone service. But I'm back in the dollhouse. I'm back with all my things."

"Yes, I heard."

Jason had said that she was living there again; the new owners had allowed her back in.

"That's great, Mom. Really, great. It must be a big relief." I was not going to allow myself to get defensive or sad or worn down by her.

"Well, yes."

There was quiet on the line. I wondered whether to tell her of my impending visit. What she or I would do with that information if I shared it. She broke the silence.

"I got your letter," she said, her voice uncharacteristically neutral.

I waited for more. I waited for her tone to change, for the litany of how I had gone wrong and thwarted her and didn't appreciate everything she'd done for me and how I was ruining myself and getting big ugly muscles and my father was a jerk and my boyfriend was not good enough...but there was no more. It seemed she didn't know what else to say.

So I said, forcing lightness into my voice, "Oh. Good. I'm glad it got to you."

There was another pause. Then she asked, "Well, so, you know, how are you?"

I was completely caught in a moment of realization that she'd never asked me this question before. This was an unprecedented moment between us. It took me a moment to collect myself enough to answer.

"Um," I said. "I'm good. Really good. I'm very happy. Thank you for asking. I'm…well, I guess I told you just about everything in the letter."

"Yes," she said. "You sound good. You sound happy." Then a pause. "I'm happy for you."

The straightforward kindness of this remark caused tears, hot and stinging, to start up and cloud my eyes.

"I'm so glad to hear that," I managed. "I'm so glad you feel that way."

"Yes. It seems you've made quite a life for yourself."

The sentence was hard for her. There was hesitation in her throat. But she also sounded sincere. It was my turn to take a risk.

"Mom."

"Yes."

"I'm coming out there next month."

"You are?" I could hear her trying to keep hope from her voice.

"Yeah. For Thanksgiving."

"Oh. You'll be visiting your father?" She was being careful.

"Yep. Jason will be there, too."

"That will be nice for you."

We waited for each other.

"Well, do you think I'll be able to see you when you're here?" She was so tentative, so childlike in her wishfulness that it broke something open in me.

"Yes, Mom. Yes. I'd like that."

"Good. I'd like to see you," my mother said. "Well, I'd better go now. I don't want to run up George's phone bill. But I'll see you soon. A few weeks. A month, I mean."

"It was good to talk to you," I said. Which was true.

"Yes," she said. "It was good to talk to you, too."

The last words my mother ever spoke to me.

Leftovers

Some years after my mother was killed, on yet another visit to my father's house in California, I went out to a storage closet in the garage. Instead of finding whatever it was I was looking for, my eyes came into focus on a large, square box with the top flaps open. I saw several neatly stacked portfolios with newspaper clippings sticking out and some wire-bound notebooks that looked vaguely familiar. I stepped into the darkness and squatted next to the box. It was filled with neat stacks of notebooks. My mother's notebooks. I was taken aback. I thought I'd been through everything that was left. I didn't know there was more, that these items were still here. I assumed they had been either destroyed or thrown away. Seeing the box was like finding a forgotten scar;

even though the wound was long numb, the memory of the original insult came back fresh and vivid. And the memory was irresistible. Here she was again, my mother, in a box of broken fragments from the past, challenging me to put her back together. I dragged the box out of the garage and into the sunlit courtyard and sat on the edge of the little koi pond my father had made and surrounded with delicately scented, white-blooming vines, roses, and shrubs. I began an excavation.

I picked up the first thing I found. It was a small, cream-colored envelope. I lifted the flap, and a curl of caramel-colored hair slid into my palm. The envelope read, in my grandmother's hand, "Anne, 1932." A lock of my mother's baby hair, so beautiful, so soft and delicate; the simple inscription so full of hope and promise. I choked back a sob as I tallied the tragedies and traumas that curl of hair had survived and my mother had not.

I slid the hair back into the envelope and picked up a black sketchbook. On the first page, in my mother's familiar hand, were the words, "Anne Ford, New York, August 1954." Then, at the bottom, under some ink stains and blots, in her handwriting, "emotional starvation and hunger." This phrase seemed so out of context. Was it written then, in 1954, when she was only in her twenties, had just won a prestigious fashion contest, moved to New York, when her world was full of opportunity? Were demons already knocking at her door, even then?

The interior pages of the book were filled with skilled and energetic sketches. There were drawings of a couple sitting cuddling in a park under a tree; some fat ladies in skirted swimsuits holding hands above the caption "Playing in the waves at Jones Beach"; a man, "Michael," reading a book; a woman, "Jane," sitting cross-legged in a full skirt and pointy shoes smoking a cigarette; a man kneeling on the floor with a pencil, and the note, "*le grand travail du* Edgar"; another man playing a guitar in a restaurant. Several pages were covered with studies of hands.

In the back were a few bawdy sketches in a different drawing style, and I recognized John Altoon's work immediately. I hadn't known that he'd been in New York with her. She'd written his name in the corner of one page. There was a delicate sketch of a face I recognized as Marlon Brando. So she hadn't lied. She'd not only dated him, she'd drawn him.

On the very last page, a self-portrait. The lines were firm, confident, and few, tracing her elegantly shaped head, droplet earrings hanging down along her long neck, the suggestion of feminine shoulders. This is the way she saw herself, I thought. Beautiful, sophisticated. Nothing in the image, nothing in any of her sketches, suggested the despair of the phrase scribbled in the front.

I set the sketchbook aside and opened a portfolio filled with yellowed pages cut from newspapers. Advertisements from the fifties showed sketches of clothing from well-known fashion labels. My mother was credited as a featured designer. Clippings from the sixties showed clothes I had seen come off the table in our house—mini dresses, suits, pants, caftans. Her name was emblazoned at the top of one page, exactly as it had appeared on her clothing label and on the carved sign that she had hung out over our front door. Headlines announced "Anne Ford's New Line for Spring."

All this success, I thought, all this opportunity. All of it gone, squandered, unsustainable.

I opened one of several spiral-bound notebooks filled with my mother's writing and sketches in entries dated from my childhood. There were even a few scattered drawings and notes in my own childish hand. I had started a letter to my father. I had written down which buses I needed to take to get to a friend's house. I'd spelled the names of the streets wrong. My mother had sketched our dog Shorty.

There were snippets of conversation: "8/6/76 Silence is Golden. J. So shut up and get rich." I could conjure the echo of this exchange, imagine my mother trying to get Jason to be quiet and then hear his witty, rude rejoinder. There were also notes about city clerks, license bureaus, and copy for signs advertising artist space for rent. It seemed she had been trying to make something happen, to come up with some sort of income, but, as usual, there was insufficient follow-though. On one page, she had written, "What I am is not because of what they say." Yes, of course, she had her own reasons for the way she was, and explanations as quotidian as excessive drink and insufficient work ethic would never have done, for her.

Another notebook held dates from the years just after I had left for New Jersey. It was filled with disjointed limericks, witticisms, and word plays. "I prefer a youth hostel to hostile grown ups." "The past is historical. The present is hysterical." "I once birthed a pussy named Dick. His uncle was named Tom Cat. Believe me he really got fat. He ate like a pig, 'till he got so big that we know exactly where he was at."

She had recorded things evocative to me precisely because of the details left out: "Jason says I am unpredictable.... The only choice is to be dictable. He feels I am not relaxed. So he is going to be violent and yell in my ear.... Mother wonders why I can't be reasonable. Hollywood High says he has to live at home with his mother." I imagined my brother trying to get her assistance on some small bureaucratic matter, to sign something for a school administrator, for example; I imagined her maddening and pointless resistance and his ensuing, understandable rage.

There was a note from November 8, 1978: "Saw Ms Covi eating and perched in her nest to discover 3 new babies sitting so adorable with 1 white egg. Now we have fifteen ducks and one friendly chicken." The damn ducks again. A complete menagerie. Her own children and everyone else had left her. The parties were over. No wonder she wanted to ducks to stay.

Another notebook opened onto this oddly spelled pronouncement: "The GOSPE according to St. Anne, 4/23/81." The first half of the book was filled with sketches of dress designs, complete with notations about style and fabrics: "Iridescent midnight blue straw hat. Navy chiffon spring afternoon gown. Beaded lilac motif, fringed lilac design purse." Almost fifteen years after she'd had her last legitimate design job, she was still designing. And her designs were still beautiful. They would remain unseen, unmade.

The second half of this book was filled, page after page, with random thoughts and observations. "When I was little I was too busy to know I was solitary. There were paper dolls and store bought dolls to tend to.... Now I am home in Hollywood where I was sought in younger days by lecherous tycoons before parades were for gays. Here we are at, as the jargon now says, alone with only my real doll's cat. My daughter remitted a book at which I cannot look because it is superficial and phony. That is not what I begat. She is manipulated and got fat from the quiet man who is her Father." These insults, more than a decade old, still wholly inaccurate, still had the power to wound me.

She wrote of Owen: "…this month is the celebration of Capricorn I squirted out of my womb 22 years ago which I lived with that knowledge all these years. A wonder he is and always will be for he is my first experience of having a baby grow so fine to give to and hardly receive. I love what he gave and hope he gives more to light up the darkness he came from."

Then of Jason: "The next I conceived was the son (sun) and the brilliance of brain was a perfect combination. I shall drink this champagne; did they name it for pain?"

And then me: "Next came a girl! My dream was a pearl—not gold nor amber nor quartz. So, she lives with a Schwartz." This, a reference to my father. The men, the pregnancies, the children: all, to her, nothing but disappointments and abandonments for which she felt victimized even as she took credit for them as her own creative acts.

The final pages of this notebook, the last record of the last part of her life, stained with water and smoke.

I looked at the things laid out around me. I had my mother's life in my hands and her voice in my head. I let the tears come and cried over everything she had been and everything she had lost. I cried over the intelligence and humor that had been retained. I cried over the illusions and delusions that sustained her. I cried because I have never been fat.

* * *

Moving things into a new house twenty years after her death, I noticed the words, "For Anne + Brent" written in the corner of an abstract painting I remembered from my childhood homes, which my father must have taken from my mother's last house, and I got after he died. The date is 1962, the year my brother was born. I suppose I had seen this note, this date, before, but it hadn't registered with me; reading it again brought forth a long-forgotten memory. Someone, it must have been my father, perhaps my brother, told me this painting was a wedding present to my parents from an artist named Pauline Annon. A wedding present. So prosaic, so lovely, a kind of memory I didn't usually associate with either of my parents.

Hanging a framed drawing that was nothing more than a set of squiggly black lines, I saw the name Craig Kauffman written in my mother's hand, on a card, stuck into the back. Another thing I had never noticed before. I started looking around more closely. I searched for but did not find any hidden signatures on the paintings by John Altoon. Of course, why would he sign something he had thrown away? I also found, among some papers, a photo sleeve with the words "Dennis Hopper's birthday party" written by my mother on the outside. There are no pictures of the famous actor inside the sleeve, just a photo of my brother and me as toddlers—he in a blue velvet suit, me in a ruffled white dress. But the discovery incited me to search out and watch *Easy Rider*. Until then, I hadn't known that Hopper also directed this iconic movie. I remembered that plaster of Paris piece of wedding cake by Claes Oldenburg. My father took it from my mother's house, and I thought my stepmother still had it. I suddenly wanted it.

I was by then old enough, and had stood in enough museums and sculpture parks, to have seen these artist's names—and those of others I could now associate with being at my mother's parties—many, many times. The evidence had mounted, and I was beginning to realize that my mother was a part of something bigger, more historic, than a decade-long party. This realization of the historical within the personal pained me because it underscored just how big the opportunity was that she missed.

I looked up "Ferus" and found this list of men's names, synonymous with the art gallery: Ed Ruscha, Craig Kauffman, Ed Kienholz, and John Altoon. Ruscha is the guy who did the Sunset Strip book I loved to fold out in the living room of the house on Fairfax Avenue. A quick search to confirm my memory shows that thirty-five years later, copies of his book are worth ten thousand dollars or more. Kauffman and Kienholz were guys in paint-spattered pants, whose artwork now shows up in museums around the world. Dennis Hopper is now known as much for his collection of 1950s and 1960s art as he is for his acting career. Ferus is considered a legendary place that nurtured a generation of radical artists, including Andy Warhol, and was immortalized in the documentary *The Cool School*. Barney's Beanery, still in its same Santa Monica and La Cienega location, is now depicted as the iconic after-hours hangout for a generation of artists and actors who defined their times. And who now are so well established in the cumulative artistic zeitgeist that they are given major retrospectives in galleries and museums around the world.

I discovered that John Altoon is better appreciated twenty, thirty, forty years after his death than while he was alive. At a 2008 show in New York, the gallery was asking thirty thousand dollars and more for his drawings and paintings. In a catalog I found from a retrospective, there were several photographs of the artist. A dark swatch of hair hung over his forehead, almost covering the thick, thoughtfully scowling eyebrows that squeezed together across the large arch of his nose. A cigarette hung from beneath a heavy moustache that stretched all the way to his jawline. He wore low-slung pants and paint-spattered shirts. He was handsome in a swarthy and brooding kind of way that to me seemed both sexy and cautionary. His face was familiar from similar photographs I had found scattered through my mother's photos.

As I read the write-ups about him and his work, many things that I had forgotten were dragged forth by their appearance on the page. He went to the Chouinard Art Institute where my mother also went, and where they met. I'd never realized the name was spelled that way. Altoon was described as "slightly mad," "possessed by real demons." My mother had told me the reason she had never married him was that he was crazy. I hadn't given credence to her estimation of him; after all, I thought, she certainly could not be considered a reliable judge of anyone else's sanity. Apparently, Altoon's fits of destruction were, in fact, legendary. He not only destroyed his own pieces but on more than one occasion tried to force his wrath on other artists' work as well.

I read that an important painting was "named for his first wife, the actress Fay Spain." I knew, in fact, adored Fay Spain, although, until now, I hadn't realized she had been his wife. I recalled the dramatic lines of her face, made more apparent by the tight bun in which she wore her ashy blond hair. I spent many days and nights at Fay's house on Malibu beach with my mother and brothers. She had a pool and, much more fascinating to me, a mynah bird that could be occasionally coaxed into a few words. We often spent the night—I recall Fay and her smooth-headed husband coaxing, cajoling my mother not to drive home after having had too much to drink. I would curl up under a soft blanket on a padded bench in a room lined with bookshelves and windows set high on stilts above the beach below. As I fell asleep, listening to the waves crashing against the sand, I would dream of a wall of water breaking through the windows and carrying me out to sea.

The catalog discussed the evolution of John's work, pointing out that as a young artist he experimented with cubism. As I read these words, I looked up at the fragmented squares and triangles of color on his painting of the flower seller hanging in my living room. The catalog went on to say that, sadly, none of his student or early works still existed. Yes, I wanted to tell someone, they do. Three of his earliest works are right here, on the dark walls of my funky farmhouse in Vermont, three thousand miles and a full lifetime away from when they were painted. I thought someone should know. I thought someone might care. I hunted around and found a curator who handled his work. He thanked me for calling but said it didn't matter; there was no "market" for student works of John Altoon. They might not have mattered to the market. But they mattered to me. Not because they were John Altoon's, but because they were my mother's.

* * *

In a conversation with my brother, I mentioned some of what I was uncovering. After decades of intermittent estrangement, in our late thirties and early forties, we began to rediscover the connection of siblings. We tiptoed back into a relationship with one another, helped along by time, distance, and the confidence new marriages and happier lives had given us both. He said he'd made scrapbooks and notebooks of his own. I asked him to send me clippings or copies of anything he thought might interest me. A few weeks later, a large manila envelope arrived. A newspaper article described the 1949 Redondo Beach Fiesta Queen: "…a lovely combination of blue eyes, brunette tresses, a Redondo tan, a—ahem—shapely figure and a sparkling personality." My mother had told the interviewer that she would put her career before men. I can only imagine how brash that must have sounded in the late forties; I was sorry she didn't stick to that promise.

There was an article from a 1953 *Glamour* magazine, her first-person recounting of the few dates she had with Marlon Brando while he was filming *On the Waterfront*. The introduction referred to her as a "dark haired gamine with big blue eyes" who "takes her career seriously (she designs blouses for a New

York manufacturer) but thinks it silly to turn down any other exciting job. This career philosophy has led so far to a spell in Hollywood playing small parts in two movies; several weeks in a Las Vegas chorus line." I had never heard about the chorus line. In the article, she recounted stories about Brando's quirks and the amusing little games he would play, how he preferred "hotdogs over highballs." The article included a sketch she did of Brando; the same one I'd seen in her sketchbook. There was an accompanying photo of her. She looked like a young Liza Minnelli, a more knowing, less delicate Audrey Hepburn. So she really did date him, I thought, smiling. I doubted so much of her, so much about her. And in so doing, I suddenly realized, missed so much of her.

There was also a clipping of an article by Geoffrey Hellman writing in the *New Yorker* a few months later. The headline exhorts my mother: "Don't Take Notes on the Boyfriend." "When a man has a date," Hellman wrote, "he sometimes says things and does things that aren't intended to be embedded in a magazine with a circulation of 603,000.... I suggest she give up blouse designing for a while, join the C.I.A., and brush up on security.... A little indoctrination at one of those secret schools in Maryland, and her beaux will breathe easier." Her little first-person narrative had inspired this commentary in a leading literary magazine. I laughed, thinking how she must have loved this attention, how much she loved any attention.

There were other articles from the mid-1960s fashion press announcing Anne Ford's latest collection as showing "color in a fluid feminine mood" and reflecting "her own young, gay personality."

Then the mood of the news clippings began to change. In 1970, a reporter described how this same fashion designer, now

216

"jobless and low on money," opened her garage for a permanent sale of everything from "furniture, toys, fabric remnants, sample dresses, pictures, beads to trunks and antiques." He writes, "Some people probably think she is a crazy lady, no longer young and not yet old, trying to exist in a somewhat Utopian world. She treats her situation as if she were a free, single young woman, not a mother with responsibilities." Yes, I thought. I was one of those responsibilities.

The last article in the stack was from 1981, and it told the story of a fifty-one-year-old woman who insisted on camping on a small lot overlooking Ventura. Neighbors complained because she "wasn't just lighting illegal fires on her property. She insisted on answering Mother Nature's calls with a visit to a next-door-neighbor's yard...." The city "cited the woman, filed a 55-count complaint against her, obtained a Superior Court order to stop her, and arrested her on suspicion of violating that order and put her in jail."

But even in these two instances, under these bizarre conditions, my mother managed to charm. The reporter who surmised that she was crazy went on to say, in typical seventies jargon, "The whole scene is obviously real and not a trip. Anne sparkles as she talks in the July afternoon heat...." The city fire inspector who cited her after repeated warnings about her campfire said, "She was going to turn this into a little Shangri-la...she seemed like a real nice lady.... It was the typical thing of the free spirit versus City Hall bureaucracy."

Of all these recorded versions of my mother, there was only one I recognized from my own experience: the failed fashion designer, the hippie hanging onto a utopian dream, the woman who refused to let go of her youth and step up to her responsibilities. But she was so many other things, before all that, before me. This delightful young woman full of talent and energy and charm was a person I never met, never knew. And now, far too late, I wished I had.

There was only one person I knew who I thought might be able to bring this earlier rendering of my mother to life for me. My mother had a cousin, Alice. We communicated from time to time, holiday cards and family updates. I remembered, as a child, visiting her home in Woodland Hills for Thanksgivings. She had a way with my mother, limiting her drink by conveniently running out of wine, changing the subject when my mother and grandmother slung veiled insults at each other, occupying me with small tasks like bringing food to the table.

I'd never asked Alice about my mother. I didn't know how she felt about her, what she knew of her. But I did know that Alice was getting older and was the only person I knew, still alive, who also knew my mother when they were both young. So I wrote. I asked her to share with me what she could, to not spare me any detail she wanted to pass along, but to spare herself anything that was upsetting or uncomfortable. She wrote back, and then she kept writing, sharing with me much more than I had hoped for or anticipated.

I didn't realize that Alice not only knew my mother from childhood but also had lived with her those years she spent in New York. Until, according to Alice, their other roommate got tired of my mother dashing off to parties leaving dishes undone and clothing scattered all over the place, and my mother moved out on her own. Alice readily told me that the actor she eventually married had his eye on my mother first. Of course, she was so beautiful, so witty, so funny, so bold, Alice said, why wouldn't he?

Alice said John Altoon had followed my mother to New York in the hopes of marrying her, but she had refused him. She said my grandparents had been brutally cruel to Altoon, referring to him as a "dirty Mexican," even though they knew his background was Eastern European. Alice shared with me many stories that illustrated my mother's much-discussed charms, her confidence, and her ability to turn almost any situation to her own advantage. She told me that after the Geoffrey Hellman article appeared, my mother called Hellman directly and introduced herself. He promptly asked her to lunch. They went somewhere "swank," and he was sufficiently enchanted by her to continue to call. My mother, put off by his age, his marriage, his lack of good looks, demurred, according to Alice.

Another time, my mother was at a party where she and a writer were regaling each other with stories of their past European romances. Well-soaked with alcohol, the writer suggested they go out to the airport, find a flight to Europe, and look up their lost loves. My mother went back to her apartment and stepped out of her coat and cocktail dress, letting them fall to the floor. She packed a small bag with a toothbrush, nightgown, and passport, and she put on a travel outfit. At the airport, they found a plane ready to return to Europe. As if finding a flight at an odd hour were implausible enough, this plane had just been relieved of a bunch of monkeys that had broken out of their crate on the ride over the Atlantic and wriggled their way into the spaces between the interior and exterior walls. Once the plane had been cleared, the ocean crossed, my mother and her new friend landed overseas and sobered up and decided to go their separate ways. He gave her some cash, she bought a matching gray sweater and skirt and traveled through France and Italy on her own, Alice recalled.

But when she returned to New York, according to Alice, she took the first of what would become a long line of missteps that could not so easily be salvaged. A friend she'd met in Italy had suggested my mother look up her soon-to-be ex-husband when she got back to the States. My mother did, and they began a serious romance. A struggling artist, he gave her a pink diamond and gold wire ring he'd made. Then he, along with three other musicians and artists, went off to Europe with the idea that they'd make it rich selling ice cream along the beach in France. Instead, they wound up broke with not even enough money to get back to the States. This is when my mother discovered she was pregnant. She wrote her penniless, not-yet-divorced beau with the news, and Alice said he responded with enthusiasm, asking about names for the baby, saying he'd be back soon to marry her. But he didn't return. And in the empty space of her waiting, a radio actor she'd met a year earlier called her up for a date. She declined, but he persisted. Finally, she broke down in tears, and when he asked what was wrong, she told him she was pregnant and abandoned. He said he'd be right over. When he got there, he told her, "Don't worry, you're going to marry me."

So she had known all along who Owen's father was. She concocted a story that both protected her lost love and gave Owen some strange hopefulness about a potentially grand provenance. I was surprised at how protective and loyal she'd been to this man she had loved, a man, like so many others, who betrayed her.

Alice said my mother called up her parents to tell her she was getting married, but to someone different from the man she'd told them about just a month earlier. Understandably, they were upset but came to New York for the wedding. She wore a simple white dress of her own design. She moved into her new husband's apartment on Gramercy Park—"she did it all over, which was completely unnecessary, but I suppose she wanted to make it her own," Alice wrote—while he went out to California, stayed with her parents, and tried to make the transition from radio to television. My mother followed at the tail end of her pregnancy. Her parents, who were by now bitterly angry and disappointed with her and her new husband, met her at the airport. Her father greeted her with a punch to the stomach and the words "Get that bastard out of here."

I had no idea my mother had suffered these insults and injuries from her parents. I began to realize that the "advantages" they gave her were better characterized as pressures that came at a terrible cost.

My mother told Alice at the time that she had confirmed her father's two worst fears: that she'd get pregnant out of wedlock and marry a Jew. I wondered if my mother knew about her father's illegitimacy and Jewish grandmother, and how these facts of his own life may have fed his two fears. Hearing this news, I felt a terrible sadness for my mother, which for the first time had nothing to do with what she had done to herself, but what others had done to her.

My mother's first marriage did not last long. Her husband could not find work, and her parents were endlessly critical and refused them help. They split up, and he died unexpectedly and young, but Alice pointed out that he gave the son, whom he'd already given his name, his residuals and an insurance policy. This was the first financial legacy that gave Owen his first chance at independence from our mother. During the course of many letters, Alice explained that during Owen's childhood, my mother got a job designing for Jantzen, one of the leading swimsuit manufacturers of the fifties and sixties. She went to work at the headquarters location in Portland, Oregon. While there, she met my father, who was finishing his senior year at Reed College.

My father had told me that he met my mother at a party he'd attended at the suggestion of a friend who had cajoled him by saying, "Oh, but you must meet Anne. She's so beautiful, so witty, so charming…she's so *superficial.*" They married and returned to California, my mother again a few months pregnant and only a few weeks married to another jobless man. At least this time, her husband, although very young, was the biological father of her child and only one-half Jewish. She continued to work for Jantzen, out of a little Laurel Canyon bungalow her parents bought and rented to her. She had a friend, Ed Kienholz—at that time a struggling rather than legendary artist—fix the garage into a sewing factory. My father took a low-paying job for a defense contractor. A year and a half after Jason was born, they had me. My father was twenty-five, my mother thirty-three. Their marriage did not last long either. By the time I was one, they were divorcing.

When, after her death, I had asked my father about their breakup, he said, "Well, you know how she was. I just came home one day, and she said she didn't want to be married anymore." He went further and said that he had asked her to go to therapy. He said she went once and then refused to continue, but he went again and the therapist told him, "Your wife is something called 'schizophrenogenic.' This is someone who makes other people around them go crazy." My father continued, "The therapist told me that if I stayed with her, I'd go nuts."

I asked him why he felt it was OK to leave two small children with her. "Back then," he said, "I wouldn't have been able to get custody of you kids. They always went to the mother. And besides, I had people watching out for you." I was not brave enough to ask and did not want to pain him by asking why he didn't at least try to get us, and whom did he have watching out for us, the people getting drunk and breaking furniture? Even then, his story rang false to me; my father always had a proclivity for dissembling and half-truths. But I didn't press him. Then, when I shared this tale with Alice, she gasped slightly before catching herself. It took her a long time to tell me her version of the story. When she did, it was clear that she'd been afraid of hurting me.

Alice said that my father had broken my mother's heart. She recalled coming by the house when my brother and I were babies and watching my father leave with a friend of my mother's, a museum curator. Alice said, "I was so naïve, I thought nothing of it." Then my father left my mother for this man. Who was also the person who introduced my young father to his friends in the museum world and thereby set my dad on what would be his only career path.

I had always wondered how my father got started in museum exhibition design. He had no education in the field and when asked was evasive. Now I had the answer. His affair could not have lasted long because some of my earliest memories of my father also include the woman whom he eventually married, my step-mother and the woman he was with until his death. But again, here was my mother protecting a man she had loved and who had abandoned her; as much as my mother railed against my father, she had never told this little secret. And the idea that my father hurt my mother in that way was amazing to me. How many times had he justified his escape from her with the simple sentence, "Well, you know how she was"? How many times had I justified his not being there for us by telling myself that he would have had to go through her? How many times had I told myself that she was the one who broke people's hearts, not the other way around?

How was it that, by the time she got to my father, she had any heart left to break?

Alice said that my mother had tried hard to make it on her own in the design world but didn't have the capital to create a full collection, and, as much as she begged, her parents wouldn't invest in her, so she was doomed to failure. It wasn't just her lack of discipline and focus; it wasn't just an unwillingness to work. Alice said my grandparents had been overly ambitious for my mother as a child, pressuring her into all the beauty pageants and contests she attended, whether she wanted to or not. And Alice told me that my grandparents had been so stingy and controlling about money that they'd gotten divorced late in life to separate their assets, even though they continued to live together. The separate bedrooms were suddenly explained. But more important, this was yet another event that hurt my mother deeply and contributed to her disgust at the penury and grasping nature of her parents.

Alice knew my mother through the last years of her life. She said that whenever my mother called her, she was always sober and always told terrific, funny stories about her life, that her spirit was indomitable, and that they always had a great laugh.

Alice knew my mother as a woman to whom life had given everything; who took those gifts and made them into things even more brilliant, more energetic, more fun; who, even when everything was taken away from her, managed to enchant not only herself but also those around her. Alice saw her not just as a bold, talented, witty woman but also as a delicate, sensitive person who was pushed into a twisted version of what might have been possible by parents who loaded her with too many of their own ambitions and men who used and abandoned her.

Parties, alcohol, giving up, became her rebellion, her self-protection. It had never occurred to me that the anger and darkness inside my mother was not innate but created by her life experiences. Of course, my mother had choices about how she responded to the pressures and disappointments of life, about how she treated those who loved her or tried to love her, but it was still a revelation to see that the sensitive child I had been was not so different, after all, from the sensitive child my mother had been.

Alice knew my mother and loved my mother throughout her entire life. Alice's memories gave to me the full woman my mother was, as well as the woman she might have been. When I thought of the woman Alice knew, I wish I'd known her, too. When I thought of the woman Alice knew, it seemed I could have loved her, too.

I wondered if it was possible to learn to love someone, even though she was impossible, and hurtful, and self-destructive, and more than a little crazy. And now long dead. I began to believe that loving my mother was not only possible but necessary.

About the Author

Photograph by Matthew Ossowski, 2011

In addition to *Unraveling Anne*, Laurel Saville is the author of four books, numerous feature articles, several short stories and essays. She earned an MFA in creative writing and literature from the Bennington Writing Seminars and has taught a variety of courses at the undergraduate and graduate level. She lives and works in the Mohawk River Valley of upstate New York. To learn more about Laurel and her newest book, visit www.LaurelSaville.com and www.UnravelingAnne.com.

Made in the USA
Lexington, KY
29 December 2011